AF771771

THE SADHUS AND INDIAN CIVILISATION

THE SADHUS AND INDIAN CIVILISATION

Vijay Prakash Sharma
M.Sc., Ph.D

ANMOL PUBLICATIONS PVT. LTD.
NEW DELHI-110 002 (INDIA)

ANMOL PUBLICATIONS PVT. LTD.
4374/4B, Ansari Road, Daryaganj
New Delhi - 110 002

The Sadhus and Indian Civilisation
Copyright © Author
First Edition, 1998
ISBN 81-261-0108-3

All rights reserved. No part of this publication may be reproduced, stored in a retrieval system or transmitted, in any form or by any means, mechanical, photocopying, recording or otherwise, without prior written permission.

PRINTED IN INDIA

Published by J.L. Kumar for Anmol Publications Pvt. Ltd., New Delhi and Printed at Tarun Offset Press, Delhi.

CONTENTS

FOREWORD

The study of religion is a critical element of the study of humankind. No other aspect of human society has incited human passions as much as has religion. Religion has moved humans to kill and destroy, to oppress and exploit, but it has also motivated humans to attain the highest moral values possible and to transcend the petty concerns which most often promote the most destructive of human behaviours. Perhaps, this is because religion, as George Santayana maintained in *Winds of Doctrine,* is the love of life in the consciousness of impotence. The struggle to love life, to reach into the depths and the heights of human possibilities, despite the awareness of the possibility of, impotence and meaninglessness, is bound to ignite the deepest of human passions. Clearly, the ability of religion to produce the best and the worst in the human spirit, makes it an essential arena for the anthropological understanding of the nature of human culture.

Professor V.P. Sharma, in this study of the ascetic tradition in Indian culture, has added to our knowledge of both religion in a particular historical-cultural context and in general. While much has been written about this tradition from an ideal perspective using textual sources, very little has been researched on the actual level of practice through fieldwork with practitioners of that tradition. By examining the ascetic life in the context of the important locale of Ayodhya and the actual practice and organisation of ascetic *muttas,* Professor Sharma exemplifies the strengths that anthropology has always brought to the study of any aspect of human culture. By focusing on a specific context, ascetic organisations in Ayodhya, he is able to weave together the complex tapestry of asceticism on the micro-level and, thus, provide concrete substance to our understanding of religious ascetics in the broader macro-level of Indian culture. And by conducting fieldwork, Professor Sharma has provided us with a picture of the actual practice of asceticism, rather than just the ideal picture painted by purely textual analysis.

While no single study can provide a complete exploration of the phenomena of religion, studies such as this one by Professor Sharma shed rays of light on this critical dimension of the human experience.

Gregory G. Reck
Visiting Professor
Ranchi University

ACKNOWLEDGMENTS

I express my gratitude to Professor L.P. Vidyarthi, who taught me anthropology and encouraged me to explore the complex world of ascetics—the vanguards of Indian civilisation through intensive field work. The preliminary enquiry was conducted in 1973 and later to detailed study was taken up in 1979. I am thankful to my teacher, Prof. V.S. Upadhyay under whose supervision this work was undertaken.

In addition to them, I had several occasions to discuss the materials on the ascetics with Prof. Agehanand Bharati of Syracuse University, Prof. Chi-Nakane of Japan, Prof. T.N. Pandey of California University, U.S.A., Prof. V.N. Mishra of Deccan College, Pune. Their suggestions have put me on the right tract in preparing this book. Prof. B.N. Saraswati and Prof. S.N. Ratha provided critical evaluation of the work. I take this opportunity to express my gratitude to them.

My special obligation goes to Gregory G. Reck, Professor of Anthropology, Appalachian State University, North Carolina, U.S.A. It was very kind of him to spare his valuable time for a critical reading of this manuscript and for contributing a learned Preface to this book, during his four months stay in India as Visiting Professor to Ranchi University.

My regards are due to Professor Bhagwan Dutta Mishra, an indefatigable scholar for his constant help in understanding the meanings of Sanskrit hymns.

My grateful thanks are due to Maharaja Jagdambika Pratap

Narayan Singh of Ayodhya and the whole 'Raj-Parivar' for their unvarying kindness to me in providing patronage during my field work at Ayodhya.

I pay my reverence to Jagadguru Ramanandacharya Sheo Ramacharya, Jagadguru Ramanujacharya Purrussottam-acharya, Paramhansa Ramchandra Das, Sri Mahanth Nritya Gopal Das, Kiladhish Sita Ram Sharanjee and all other ascetics of Ayodhya for their invaluable help and co-operation.

I am thankful to Prof. S.K. Chaudhury, Department of English for useful corrections in the manuscript.

On the other side of the hill my wife Manju and my sons Mrigank and Shashank kept me agile.

No book can ever be the product of a single person, and there are many who share in the credit for making this effort a reality. I am thankful to Sri Ram Autar Prasad for typing the manuscript. The staff at Anmol Publications Pvt. Ltd., New Delhi deserves special credit for care, caution and elegance in publication of this book.

V.P. Sharma

1

INTRODUCTION

History in India has a special character of its own: the course of its evolution is guided by the religious leaders—the ascetics. Here the summum-bonum of life is liberation, i.e., the complete cessation of the cycle of life and birth. This has been designated as the Parampurusartha or the highest of life. According to the Indian thought Moksha or liberation is the highest and the best of the four Purusartha i.e. Dharma Artha, Kama and Moksha. Various means and ways have been suggested here for the attainment of the same. Baldeo Upadhyay has observed that "the Indian culture is based upon the three T's—Tyag (renunciation), Tapasya (penance) and Tapovan (hermitage), (Upadhyay, 1953). It means that the ancient sages of India observed remarkable penance in their hermitages with renunciation of the worldly objects and attraction in order to achieve the highest state of knowledge. Thus, it is clear that the ascetics played a very important role in the shaping of culture here and in guiding general mass in the process of leading life. As such ascetic organisations have their own importance in Indian social setup and their history has a remote past. Dharma played an important role and ascetics from the very beginning have been defining, describing, explaining and guiding the Dharma principle for the Indian life. This placed them on the highest social platform and even the emperors have bowed down before them, showed great respect to them and made proper arrangement for them. Goodness and virtue are sine-qua-non for the attainment of highest knowledge and all these aspects of Indian life have been contributed by the ascetics.

If we look back to the history of the Indian civilisation, we find that Dharma had pervaded all aspects of India's creative life. It is evident that the ancient ascetics in their organisations have endowed the performances of excellence. Mention may be made of Manu, Yagyavalkya, Parasar, Panini and Sushrut.

Professor N.K. Bose observed in an important article published in 1951, that the institution of asceticism (Sanyasa) provided a safety valve of individual liberty against the pressures of rigid hierarchic caste system:

"India has been, however, a land in which, in spite of regimentation in many matters, the freedom of the individual was held Supreme good... there was, however, one condition attaching to the freedom: it was given only to those who were prepared to pay a heavy price for it... He had to surrender all the benefits normally derived from collective life: he had to live upon minimum of clothes, have no roof over his head, and to be constantly on the move. He was to become God's beggar and in order to enter into the Sanyasa the individual had to perform the last rites of Shradha for his own Soul. The Sanyasin was put beyond the normal operations of social, laws? (Bose 1951).

Professor Surjeet Chandra Sinha opines that "a proper understanding of the social organisation of the Hindu Civilisation would be incomplete without an adequate study of the complementary organisation of the ascetics, not only as an ideal model but as real organisations operating on the ground... proper understanding of the sources of strength of Indian civilisation will have to be based on deep probing into the complementary roles of the world's of ascetics and that of the laity guided by the Varna-Jati rules... for, civilisation, by definition, is the cultivation of excellence... we, are interested not only in the science of human system but also the art of human organisation. And so long as anthropology is cribbed and confined within the conventional limits of natural science, it will never be a mirror for the finer aspect in man." (Sinha and Saraswati, 1978).

Progress in anthropological researches in the 19th Century aroused much interest in ancient religions. Hopkins observed that "the Hindu religions should be studied with the purpose to know the manner in which religious and theistic ideas arose and developed among people, and the light these shed on the origin and development of such ideas elsewhere" (Hopkins: 1895, 565-5).

The first article appeared on Bhagwatism, Narayaniya and Bhagvatas by Grierson, who also contributed to the *Encyclopaedia of Religion and Ethics* in an essay on Bhaktimarg—the Vaishnavite—doctrine of Devotion (Grierson 1908, 1913). A monograph Vaishnavism, 'Shaivism and Minor Religious System' by Mr. R.G. Bhandarker is an outstanding work in this field (Bhandarker, 1913). Mr. Brajendra Seal expressed his conviction that "Vaishnavism was eminently suited, to contribute very valuable elements to the European Renaissance of 20th Century" (Seal, 1913). Mr. R.P. Chanda made an attempt to re-construct the early history of Vaishnavism on the basis of archeological records (Chanda, 1920).

A significant trend has emerged in Indian Anthropology to study both the non-traditional and traditional cities as well as the Hindu-Tirtha etc. In encouraging a sophisticated study of both Heterogenetic and Orthogenetic Cities, Robert Redfield and Milton Singer provided a Methodology by publishing their paper "The Cultural Role of Cities" (Redfield and Singer, 1941-51). This paper provided stimulations and direction to the Urban studies in India like Kashi, Myth and Reality of a Classical Cultural Tradition (Saraswati, 1973),

Sacred Complex of Kashi (Vidyarthi, 1978).

The first sociological enquiry, Indian Sadhu was published by G.S. Ghurye (Ghurye, 1953). Another sociological work was published by B.D. Tripathi named Sadhus of India (Tripathi, 1978). The first anthropological exploration. Ascetics of Kashi by Surjeet Sinha and B.N. Saraswati provides a good account of the ascetics of Kashi, but in the author's words—"Nor would we go for intensive and ethnographic study of a single monastic group as participant observers" (Sinha and Saraswati 1978). In the present venture I have, therefore, limited my sphere of study to a single monastic sect called Vaishnavite with special reference to Ramananda at Ayodhya.

Definitions

Asceticism: Asceticism is derived from the Greek word Akoknois meaning training. The athelete was one trained, and so one might be an athelete in virtue as well. So, very early the ascetic became the spiritual athelete of Church history. Two quite different conceptions mingle in the history of asceticism. One of these preserves the original meaning of discipline of the body for some ultimate purpose. The other conception distrusts the body altogether. Asceticism has as its function not the training but the disciplining of the body or negation of its importance (Hall, 1905, 63).

Indian Asceticism: In India, spiritual sufferings gave rise to a pantheistic world view, with dispair and asceticism as characteristic features. The forms of this asceticism are those of world of flight, the hermit life, the mortification of the body by unnatural inhibitions of all its desires. The most imperative of these was the sexual impulse, as it was also linked with the continuance of the hated existence, the mortification of this impulse became primary. The asceticism of Brahmanism and with an absorption into God. It was a training for spiritual-vision (Geden, 1909).

Ascetics: There are various terms used for ascetic in spiritual Sanskrit texts, other texts as well as in common usages:

According to Sir Monier Williams, the Sanskrit equivalent words of ascetics are Vanprastha, Tapaswi, Vairagi, Yogi, Tapas, Muni, Yati, Sanyasi and Parikanchni (Williams, 1883).

According to *Vishnu Purana* there are three kinds of

Rishis

(1)	*Brahmrishi*	:	Ascetics who are the sons of Brahma as Marichi, Atri, Vasishta etc., dwelling in the sphere of Brahma.
(2)	*Deorishi*	:	Ascetics, who are also demi gods as Narad, Nar-Narayan, Kardabh, dwelling in the region of the God.
(3)	*Rajarishi*	:	L Royal ascetics or holy personages who are also kings or the men of military class and who have attained the rank of Rajrishi from the practice of religious austerities. Such were Ikshwaku, Vishwamitra, Pururava, Dushyant etc. Their sphere is the heaven of Indra (Tr. Wilson, II ed. 1961).

In *Amarkosh*—four other class of Rishis are enumerated namely:

(1)	*Maharshi*	:	A great ascetic such as Vyas, the arranger of Veda.

(2) *Paramarshi*	:	Most excellent ascetic such as the Munivel, the author of some medical works.
(3) *Kandarshi*	:	Ascetics who teach a particular Kand (section) of the Vedas as Gemini.
(4) *Shrutarshayan*	:	Inspired ascetics as the author of medical works called Sushrut etc. (Ed. Sharma, 1941).

The world Saint of ascetic has been used by many scholars to denote a wise, pure, noble, one who sacrifices his life for the good of others, the moralist and one who remains calm and quite.

Dr. Radhakrishnan has explained that "one who takes to Sanyas, gives up his entire property and keeps himself aloof from the caste differences and religious actions, because he makes himself perfect. A Sanyasi or ascetic holds the view that the entire universe is his place and his only religion is to do good to others. A Sanyasi or ascetic is a ultra social man, is a Parivrajak a moving teacher who always influences the spiritual ideals although he keeps himself aloof from the society. He neither belongs to a particular language nor to a particular caste, but he belongs to himself and he puts himself for the entire universe." (Radhakrishnan 1970 416-20). The term Ascetic has been used with its different synonyms in the present treatise with all its meanings to denote a particular type of people at Ayodhya, initiated into the fold of Vaishnava Sampradaya and commonly called Vairagi.

Evolution of Indian Asceticism

Any diachronic study covering reasonable span of time needs to be categorised in terms of reflective chronological phases of evolution. Though, there is great controversy among historians in putting history of Indian Civilisation in chronological order due to the fact that Hindu writers went to one extreme in ignoring history altogether, they care more for truth of experience or the soundness of doctrine than for the circumstances that gave it birth. But many historians and indologists have speculated the issue on the basis of some convenient land marks in the history of India. One such attempt was made by D.S. Sharma (1961) to give a historical sketch of Hinduism. On the basis of his divisions of history of Hinduism into periods, an attempt has been made here to determine different evolutionary phases of Indian Asceticism, which will help us to understand anthropologically, the evolution of this particular trait of Indian Civilisation from its simple to complex form.

Here, my humble venture is to place Indian Asceticism into phases equating with historical age. These seven phases constitute:

1. Formative Phase — 2000 B.C. to 1000 B.C.
2. Normative Phase — 1000 B.C. to 500 B.C.
3. Propogative Phase — 500 B.C. to 300 A.D.
4. Monotheistic Phase (orthodox) — 300 A.D. to 1400 A.D.
5. Reformative Phase — 1400 A.D. to 1750 A.D.
6. Activistic Phase — 1750 A.D. to 1950 A.D.
7. Integrative Phase — 1950 A.D. onwards

Though, there are clear cut demarcations of these phases but for continuity overlapping cannot be overlooked.

I. *Formative Phase:* This phase is the phase of origin of Asceticism in India and compilation of 'Rigveda'. It can safely be placed in the beginning period of Vedic Age which is also called the Age of *Mantras.* During this phase we find the beginning of worship of half personified forces of nature to realisation of absolute spirit was in practice. The enumerated ascetics of this phase are 'Madhuchandas, Gritsamad, Atree, Bharadwaj and Vashista. The phase clearly transpires that asceticism evolved during this phase with the introduction *Ashrama* theory for individuals life. This theory placed the asceticism as fourth phase of life. This phase can be equated with historical chronology approximately from 2000 B.C. to 1000 B.C.

II. *Normative Phase:* The second phase of Asceticism which I have named normative phase also find its place in the second and third part called Age of Brahmins and Upnisads respectively of the vedic age. Here we find a number of ascetics like Aitreya, Shandilya, Pipalada, Janaka, Yagyavalky Agastya, Kapila, Valmiki and Vyas. This phase witnessed crystallisation of different norms of asceticism in the form of Upanishads. The nucleus of Ramayana and Mahabharata appeared alongwith the grammar of Yaska and Panini. The highest truth of Hinduism were discovered and the principal Upanishadas that formed the basis of Hindu philosophy appeared. Mahavira and Buddha appeared with their new doctrine of asceticism. Their doctrines are now known as Jainism and Buddhism respectively. The Ashrama theory introduced informative phase was adopted as social norm placing asceticism on its fourth stage. This idea of *Ashrama* began to take shape in the minds of people and were widely accepted as social norms for individuals. This phase can be dated from 1000 B.C. to 500 B.C. A very complex ritualism developed 'Vishnu' and 'Rudra' become important deities. Elaborate ritualistic treatises called the 'Brahmanas' are produced by the ascetics under the guidance of their Chief Aitareya. Death of 'Budha' marks the end of this phase.

III. *Propogative Phase:* This phase starts with the

systematisation of 'Vedangas' and 'Sutras' by the ascetics like Gautama, Apastamba, Ashwalayana etc. Monk life and Monastry system for ascetics were introduced in Budhism which came into great prominence. Ascetics were being sent to all parts of India, Cylon, Burma, Syria and Egypt under Budhism. The gate of asceticism were opened for general mass which were only individualistic in nature in previous two phase. Vaishnavism and Shaivism developed into ascetic cults in the fold of Hinduism. The ascetic life become the crown of the religious life during this phase. It was propagated vehementally that if one wants 'Nirvana' one must quit the world and become 'Sanyasin'. Ascetics were placed on highest platform of society. The Emperors accepted their authorities and made all arrangements for them. After the end of the Mauryan rule a new renaissance made Hinduism more popular. The 'Smritis' appeared compiled by the ascetic 'Manu' and the disciples of Yagyav kya. With the appearance of Jaimini and Vadrayan the philosophical sutras of various kinds were clearly distinguished into six schools of philosophy. The old stories of Ramayana and Mahabharat enlarged and popularised. The Sectarian formation of asceticism cristalised. Budhist ascetics divided into two sects Mahayana and Hinyana and Jain ascetics into Digambara and Swetambara. Others into Vaishnava and Shaiva sect.

This phase virtually witnessed the propagation of asceticism to whole of Asia, Syria and Egypt. This way Indian asceticism broken the boundary of nation and assumed universalistic shape. The phase ended with the rise of Gupta empire. The period can be estimated from 500 B.C. to 300 A.D.

IV. *Monotheistic (Orthodox) Phase:* The estimated period of this phase falls between 300 A.D. to 1400 A.D. This phase patronised by Samudragupta witnessed the popularisation of Hindu Dharma through religious poems known as Puranas.

The spirit of sectarianised asceticism becomes more and more aggressive leading towards a sort of sectarian monotheism intolerant of other faiths. Vaishnavism, Shaivism and Shaktism became the most important sects. The sectarian orthodoxy developed gradually through Puranas and Sutras. The rituals for different sects were distinguished.

Two great Ascetics like Kumarilla and Shankaracharya appeared and gave final blow to Budhism, reviving vedic rituals, rites and ceremonies. Shankra continued the millitant activity of Kumarilla and established his four famous monasteries as centres of religious organisations. He was a great champion of the orthodox faith and an ardent reformer. He encouraged all the forms of purer worship. Alwars and Nayanars in south joined hands to dethrone Jainism in south. Millions of people joined ascetic fold. D.S. Sharma writes, "Shankaras philosophy was a remarkable intellectual achievement, while the movement was an extraordinary overflow of heart. In both Vaishnavism and Shaivism we have first a school of mystic and saints who composed devotional songs in the vernacular and then, at a later stage, a school of philosophers who created theisic system of thought." (Sharma 1961, 37).

The Alwars and Nayanars started Bhakti movement in Vaishnavism and Shaivism respectively. Five schools of Bhakti arose those of Nimbarka, Madhva, Vishnushwami, Vallabha and Chaitanya. The Avatar (incarnation) theory of Vishnu popularised.

In the second part of this phase we find many ascetic cults arose in Shaivism and Vaishnavism under their miraculous teachers, which are dealt separately in second and third chapter of the text. The great Vaishnava ascetic Ramanujacharya and Vedantdesik appeared. Their followers are known as Acharyas. The Alwars were mystic and poets whereas the Acharyas were scholars and thinkers. The Yamunacharya established the orthodoxy of the pancharatra school, refuted Shankaras doctrine of *Advaita.* Ramanuja errected his edifice of *vishishtadvaita* on the foundation laid by Yamunacharya. Ramanuja became the most popular ascetic of eleventh century A.D. Next to him was vedantdesika who wrote profusely in Sanskrit as well as in Tamil. The followers of these schools in Northern India were in every may more conservative and orthodox than their counterparts in Southern India. The Northern asceticism only initiated higher caste people and were opposed to giving all the previledges of initiation to the lower castes. This phase is supposed to be concluded with the invasion of Timur at the end of 14th century.

V. *Reformative Phase:* The invasion of Timur at the end of fourteenth century till the fall of Moghul empire in 1707 A.D. was a period of great upheaval for Hinduism. The tyranny of Timur and Aurangzeb's staunch favour to spread to Islam in this country united Hindus under Shivaji, which later established Maratha power under the banner of Hinduism. In between Timur and Shivaji a religious and social upheaval was created by saints and poets who sprang from the lower orders of society. A great Bhakti movement began under Ramananda and swept over Northern India with the result that there was an outburst of devotional literatures. This movement brought reform by breaking the orthodoxy propagated by Sankara and Ramanuja. Ramananda, was the follower of Ramanuja, but he went to Benaras and established his new sect. He recognised no caste distinction among his followers. He had twelve disciples at first including an outcaste and even a Mohammedan. Mohammedan disciple was Kabir, who become a great ascetic afterward. The influence of Ramananda spread in various parts of the country. His followers in direct line of descent were called Ramanandis. This reform movement was further carried on by his disciples like Kabir, Nanak, Tulsidas etc. One of his disciple Ramdas become instrumental in encouraging Shivaji to establish Maratha empire, spreading Hindu philosophy. In addition, man other ascetics like Jnaneshwar, Namdev, Eknath, Tukaram etc. appeared. Vallabhacharya and Chaitanya attracted man followers. These ascetics created a new ground and popularised the ascetic norms with reforms among the masses. The process of initiation into asceticism was simplified only to a *mantra* and a sacramental meal. The institution of sectarian order of Sanyasins created. The relaxing of the rules of caste, some time even ignoring all caste distinctions and religious teachings through vernacular started.

Guru Govind Singh organised his followers into a militant group to oppose the Muslim power. The 'Naga' Sanyasins and Vairagis were also organised into militant groups under Madhusudan Saraswati and Swami Balnand respectively to fight against Islamic force. With the reform movement Indian asecticism assumed a new social role. This way the entire medieval period of Indian history can be looked as Reformative phase of Asceticism which further paved the way to social activistic role of ascetics.

VI. *Activistic Phase:* In this phase various ascetic organisations like *Dwaragadi, Akhara, Matha* and *Sthanas* were established by different ascetic sects. The ascetics took lead in mass awareness through *Ramayana* preaching and organising *Yajna* in distant rural villages of India. The ascetic organisations involved themselves in social services. Ascetic leaders like Ramkrishna Paramhansa and his disciple Swami Vivekanands spread the message of social uplift. Vivekananda emerged as the champion compaigner of Indian ascetic philosophy. He not only made the Indians aware about the underlying truth of asceticism but also spread it to America and Europe. The Rama Krishna Mission, for teaching Hinduism and doing social work was established. Swami Aurbindo established him Ashrama of Yoga in Pondicherry to teach the philosophy of supermind and integral yoga. Many ascetic organisation of Ayodhya engaged themselves in establishing Sanskrit Colleges, Hospitals, Libraries for public benefit. They developed a largest network of disciples throughout the country for social services. Many ascetics like Baba Ramcharan Das and Banda Vairagi, with their followers participated in freedom movement. This way the Activistic phase in Indian asceticism continued till 1950 A.D.

VII. *Integrative Phase:* With the Indian independence, a new trend in asceticism emerged. This have been placed as integrative movement of all ascetics cults. *The Sanyasins and Vairagis* who in past fought many times for their superiority, joined hands together for the cause of Ramajanmabhoomi at Ayodhya. The Ascetic leaders of various cults came into close interaction motivated by Vishwa Hindu Parisad, Bharat Sadhu Samaj, and many political parties. The four Shankaracharyas were accepted as the official Spokesmen of Hindu views by the Government of India. The Great battles of Shiva and Vaishnava is over. Ascetics of all cults i.e. *Shaiva, Vaishnava, Shakta, Nathpanthi* etc. developed inter-group dialogue and joined common platform. Many of them joined national politics with the idea that politics must be governed by religious piousness. This integration is developing by leaps and bounds. One has to wait and see the results and new directions of Asceticism in India. The establishment of Hare-Krishna Society to spread the message of peace and tranquillity to entire world is a new landmark in the history of Indian asceticism. The growing popularity of this society in America and Europe has opened a new page in Indian Asceticism.

Some Techniques and Methods Applied

For the understanding of man and his civilisation, an anthropologist follows various methods and applies a number of techniques. The field method used in this study are those current anthropological reporting through participant and non-participant observation, interviewing various ascetics and others and to check data given by informants. The main techniques or methods applied are as follows: This study is based on intensive field work, conducted first in 1973 then in 1979 employing synchronic and dychronic approaches.

Establishing Rapport

Before starting the study of the locality the investigator feels it necessary to establish friendship or goodwill with the people of the particular locality to get correct and broad information. The success of a field anthropologist depends largely on the ability to establish rapport in the field. It is easy to establish rapport in simple societies i.e. tribe by participating in their festivals, by taking liquor or by sitting with them for gossiping. But in the complex society of these ascetics it is very difficult. No doubt there is a superiority feeling among the ascetics. They do not want to talk with the person who does not show respect to them by bowing down his head or by saying Dandwat Maharaj. The Mahanths were impressed with my knowledge of different Shastric performances and the recitation of various prayers to deities in Sanskrit impressed them most. I had decidedly the advantage of being a Brahmin of Gaya District of Bihar. I fully utilised my caste identity with Brahmin informants of Ayodhya and developed a territorial affinity with the ascetic informants.

I confess that I had to bow down my head before the Mahanths but I always tried to maintain a respectable distance from other ascetics and non-ascetic informants. I deliberately avoided style of showing such respect to ascetics in general. On several occasions I felt dejected as I was not treated well by some informants. But all these sufferings and humiliations disappeared the moment I was treated congenially by other informants.

Survey of Ascetic Organisations

For the purpose of this study, the entire city of Ayodhya was surveyed by the moving from ward-to-ward, each road and lane. Finally a list was prepared after untiring efforts of ten days. With the help of this survey a list of 93 Ascetic organisations was prepared. These organisations were classified into two groups Ramanujee and Ramanandi. Out of these ascetic organisations, 8 organisations (6 of Ramanandi and 2 of Ramanujee) were selected as sample for holistic study because of the similarities in their organisation, routine, functions etc.

Use of Native and Sanskrit Terms

As the ascetic life pattern is based on the principles described in Sanskrit texts, the Sanskrit terms have been used in this study.

Whenever, the work is done by means of common language the investigator soon finds it impossible to keep away from the native terms. There are many native terms that have no direct English equivalant word. We have mentioned all those terms in the book and their English explanation is given in glossary at the end of the treatise which would help the reader to understand the respective phenomena.

Interview: To get the data from different ascetics of their personal life, We had to depend on individual interview because the informants did not agree to say any thing about their ascetic life in the presence of others. We interviewed several learned persons to get information on almost all the aspects of my study by asking direct and simple questions. Sometimes, judging the mood and attitudes of the interviewees, We started gossiping without putting any question and picked up many relevant informations. Learned Mahanths were interviewed to know the texual explanations of different organisations and the interview with the general ascetics provided the contextual details. The advocates of Faizabad were also interviewed to get the cases of litigations etc. connected with Ascetic organisations.

Observation: Through this method informations on daily activity of the people, behaviour of the people etc. were collected. Observation method was applied in two ways: by participating i.e. participant observation and by non-participating i.e. non-participant observation method. In my field, I had observed a varried number of situations and phenomena. Participation with the permission of my informants helped me much in collecting informations on the ceremonies like Bhandara, Diksha, Bharat-Yatra etc. It also acquainted me with the activities of the Sadhus through day and night. It was a pleasant moment when I was accepted by the ascetics very kindly to live with them for a year.

Written Records

Help is taken from the written records about income and expenditure of the organisation and also had gone through the court documents, old Mafinamas at organisations, District Gazetteers and Sanskrit texts.

Photography: A good photographic record is an essential part of Anthropological field work. Photographs also illustrate the facts. Some photographs were taken of different aspects of an ascetic's life and various ascetic organisations at Ayodhya.

Life History and Case Study

Life histories are interesting than ordinary historical accounts as they do not contain the dry narration of the facts. The feelings and viewpoints of the narrator pass like a thread in the garland through out the narration and the personal touch provides life to the events. They contain some innermost secrets unknown to the people. They are also helpful in knowing the feelings and reactions of the person relating to various kinds of events and thus provides an interesting psychological study. They are also true and therefore, more reliable. I had taken 50 life histories of ascetics. Through a systematic sociological interpretation of life histories of the people we can understand the process of socialisation and personality formation, various facts and events, customs and traditions of their societies. I have taken 50 life histories and tried to throw light on motivational causes that changed the general life of individual into ascetic. Case study is a method of exploring and analysing the life of a social unit, be that a person, a family, an institution, a cultural group or an entire community. Case studies were taken to know the different events and also to know the legal cases against the ascetics and their organisations.

2

AYODHYA: THE CITY OF RAMA

Nomenclature of Ayodhya

Ayodhya being an old place has the grace of finding expression in many literature, but with different names. Here it is apt to mention some of the names used by different authors in their writings about Ayodhya which are of course very old.

Maharshi Valmiki has described Ayodhya in *Balkanda* of *Valmiki Ramayana* as a capital of Kosala.

Valmiki described Ayodhya at the time of Rama's rule as a very prosperous city, the people of which were healthy, wealthy, and truthful. The kingdom of Kosala was situated along the side of river Saryu. The City of Ayodhya was decorated with many *Mahapatha* (road around the city) and central Rajmarga with a magnificent, huge *Rajprasad* Ramkot with four gates. None of such descriptions are evidenced now.

Tulsidas in his Ramcharita Manas has mentioned Ayodhya as the capital of Rajya of Koshal (Balkanda 123 Sarg, Shloka 1). Ramkrishna Bhandarker of Bombay has written in his *History of Decan* that Koshal was a Rajya near Vindhya Parvat. And as in *Vayupurana*, Kusha was designated as the King of Koshal who used to live at Kushsthali on Vindhya Parvat, Ayodhya must be the capital of Uttar Koshal, situated on the bank of river Saryu.

In Bauddh Granthas, Ayodhya is described as Saket or Vishakha; Saket because it has come by itself, hence famous as Saket and Vishakha on account of the following story—Vishakha was the daughter of a Trader, named Dhananjoy of Rajgrih. Dhananjoy married to Purnavardhan of Saket. Vishakha, was the first to accept Buddhism and established a Matha of Buddhdev at Saket known as Puravaram, where Buddhadev stayed for 16 years, so, people of Buddha period began to call Ayodhya as Visakha.

Fa-Hien, who came to India during the period of King Chandra Gupta II in the 5th century A.D. used the word Sanchee (Chinese translation of Saket) for Ayodhya in his famous travellogue. He also mentioned a tree near Datun Kund. Another Chinese Pilgrim, Yuan-Chawang, who visited India in the 7th century A.D. after travelling more than 600 Li and crossing the Ganges to the South. He says that Ayodhya is Saketa i.e. Ayodhya. (Law: 1954).

Hium tsang visited India during the reign of Harsha-Vardhana, wrote about two cities, named Sanchi and Pisokia (Chinese translation for Ayodhya) which are linked but are two separate cities. He too mentioned the tree near Datun Kund.

Some people believe that Saket and Ayodhya were two different places and Rhys-Davids (*Buddhist India*, p. 39) had gone to the extent of saying that in Buddha period these two cities were existing. Cunningham (Ancient Geography of India—page 493) had opined that Saket (the word used by Kalidas for the city near Saryu) and Pisokia denotes the same city of Ayodhya. For this he had cited the example of Datun Kund. It is said that Rama used to wash his teeth with Datun of a special tree here at Ayodhya. It is also said that Buddha had lived at Saket for 16 years, where he had planted a tree which was seven feet high. The tree was described by Fa-Hien and Hien-Tsiang at a place called Sanchee and Pisokia respectively. Again, according to the Chinese travellers the circumference of Pisokia was 144 lee, which was exactly what Cunningham viewed that is of 24 miles. According to Chaudah Kosi Parikrama, the circumference of sacred Ayodhya is about 28 miles, which is quite approximate to the above statement. This should settle the question that Saket and Ayodhya or Pisokia are the same.

Other names used for the town are Ikshvaku Bhumi (Prachin Bharat Ke Aitihasik Bhugol by Bimal Chandra Laha, of Uttar Pradesh, Hindi Grantha Academy), on the name of its first ruler, Ikshvaku, and Rampuri because Ayodhya became famous as a religious centre on account of mythological figure Rama).

Ayodhya in the Historical Perspective

The history of any old place can be studied with reference to three different periods: Ancient history, Medieval history and Modern history. The history of Ayodhya makes it clear that it is a very old city where Hindu religion flourished irrespective of time and nature of the ruling dynasty.

Ancient History of Ayodhya

The first ruler of Ayodhya, the capital of Koshala, was said to be Ikshvaku, the eldest son of Manu, and the first in the line of Suryavanshi Kings. According to Epics, this Ikshvaku dynasty of Suryavanshi Kings made a very important contribution to the ancient glory of India. Of the 125 Kings of this line said to have ruled at Ayodhya, 94 reigned prior to the end of Mahabharata and the rest after it, the main line ending in about the 9th Century B.C. (Gazetteer, page 28).

Among the Suryavanshi Kings the most famous were Raja Prithu (6th of the line) from whom the earth derived its name Prithvi; Raja Harishchandra (31st of the line famous for his truthfulness; Raja Dashratha (63rd of the line) father of Rama, Ramchandra (64th of the line) famous for his ideal Ramrajya etc. Rama's life was so perfect that Hindus regard

Him as incarnation of Lord Himself. Raja Kusha son of Rama, transferred the capital of the Kingdom from Ayodhya to Kush-Sthali, the place at the foot of Vindhya range. From this moment Ayodhya became vitally and virtually deserted and never had the opportunity to re-assert its previous eminence.

Five of the 24 Jain Tirthankars were born here, and Gautam Buddha stayed here for quite a long time about 16 years. These facts added dimension to the religions and sacred land-scape of Ayodhya. Pandit Umapati Tripathi (A learned man of Ayodhya) stated that a Stone inscription was found at Mani-Parvat which was sent to Lucknow by Badshah Nasiruddin (though presently there is no evidence of it). On it was written that Stupa (where Mani-Parvat IS) was built by Nanda-Vardhana, Maharaj of Magadha. In history there are two Nand-Vardhanas—first belonged to Pradyot Kul, who died in 782 B.C. Most of the scholars like Cunningham etc., believed that Stupa at Mani-Parvat was established by Nand Vardhana of Shishunak Vansha. Whoever the establisher might have been, there is ample evidence that a Bauddh sacred centre (once) existed at Ayodhya.

By the beginning of Sixth Century B.C., Kashi Kingdom was annexed by King Mahakosala of Koshala: and the two Kingdoms were divided into North and South Koshala, demarcated by river Saryu and with Shravasti becoming the capital of North Koshala and Kushavati of South Koshala, Ayodhya had sunk into insignificance.

Then came the Nanda period, Mahapadmananda killed the successor of Nanda Vardhana and reigned for 88 years on Koshal (Part of Magadh) since 422 B.C. But his eight sons ruled only for 12 years and on account of the efforts of Chanakya. The Maurya Dynasty was established in 322 B.C. By 189 B.C., Pushya Mitra, a Brahmin general of last Maurya King assassinated his master and established Shunga Dynasty, which lasted till 75 B.C. A hoard of copper coins recovered from Ayodhya in 1865 revealed that Shunga dynasty ruled Ayodhya about the second and first Centuries B.C., this proves the statement made earlier.

The restoration of Ayodhya must be credited to the King Vikramaditya of Ujjain, who usually is identified with Chandra Gupta Vikramaditya (379-413 A.D.). There is a famous legendary story behind this, which will be dealt with later on. It is also said that Vikramaditya had built about 300 temples at Ayodhya. But only Janma-Bhumi built by him is present now and that also in the shape of Mosque built in 16th century. As the Gupta's power declined, Ayodhya (called at the time—Saket) also began to fall into a state of desolateness.

Again one finds a legendary story that Raja Vikramaditya had reigned for 80 years at Ayodhya. After that Yogi Samudrapal, who had caste off his Atma (the soul) from his body and entered into it, himself began to govern this Kingdom. It is said that these Yogis had reigned for about 643 years, (17 generation) from 480 A.D. to 1123 A.D. But it appears incredible as there is no historical evidence of it.

Ayodhya was under Kanuj Raja in Harshavardhana's time, i.e. from 601 A.D. to 647 A.D. (the coins found in Bhataura village of Faizabad district, carry Prajapati and Shiladitya stamps, which were assigned to Prabhakar Vardhana and Harshavardhana by Sir Richard Burn. According to the famous Chinese Pilgrim Hien-Tisang, Ayodhya at the time of Harsha possessed about 100 Buddhist monastries, more than 3000 Mahayani and Hinayani monks and only ten Deva (Non-Buddhist God) temples.

In the 10th Century A.D., Chandradev Gaharwar defeated Parihars and during this period Saiyad Salar Masud Gazi attacked Avadh and was killed in Baharaich. Jayachandra was the last King of Gaharwar Dynasty, and in 1195 after his death in the war against Muhammad Shaihabb-U-din-Ghori, the Hindu Rajya ended and the Turks occupied Kanauj including Ayodhya thereafter.

History of Medieval Period

In first Muslim Invasion (ascribed to Ghazi Miyans) sometimes before 1030 A.D., Gazi Miyan is said to have come upto Baharaich. Kanak Bhawan of Ayodhya is stated to have been ruined by Gazi Miyan according to the temple's organisers.

At the time of war (1195 A.D.) between Ghori and Prithviraj, Ayodhya was in the hands of Gaharwars of Kanauj and after that Ayodhya was captured by the Muslims. And it was Bakhtiyarkhilzi, who made Ayodhya the Centre of Avadh state and made it an army Centre.

There continued to be many successors and challengers to the Kingdom of Avadh (Ayodhya) giving rise to much instability. In the reign of Balbans the ministers at Ayodhya were many and they all had misbehaved in one way or the others. Swami Ramanand also made his appearance at Ayodhya and his disciples reverted many Muslims into Hindus at this time.

Then came the Tuglak Dynasty. In Parrekh Firokshahi it is written Muhammed-Bin-Tuglak had built a City on the bank of Ganges and he named it Swargdwars (the present Swargdwar). Firoz Tuglak visited Ayodhya in 1324 and 1348 A.D. (Sitaram 1952).

While Sikandar Lodi ruled, peace prevailed in Avadh but his successor Ibrahim Lodi failed to preserve order. It was Babur, who after rebelling against the Afghan Chiefs regained Avadh (Ayodhya was its capital) by 1528 A.D. and enthroned himself as Emperor. He was the one who turned Janmabhumi temple into a Mosque at the request of Fakir Fazal Abbal Kalandar and Ashikan Mushake, whose blessings in his childhood enabled him to rule and conquer vast stretches of land. But his successors could not keep his empire intact and references to Avadh became very scanty in the following chronicles. Yet it is believed that the province of Avadh was famous for its excellent rice cultivation and good harvests. Most of the governors were not however worthy of mentioning. Safdar Jang, Prime Minister Nawab Rai of Itawa is said to be the builder of Nageshwar Nath temple of Ayodhya. In the Mughal period the names of different areas of Ayodhya was changed into Muslim names as given in Appendix-V.

By 1765 A.D. along with victorious ascent of the East India Company, Clive had strengthened Avadh as a buffer state between Bengal and Northern India and restored the Districts of Avadh to Shiraja-Ud-Daulah.

Faizabad was soon replaced by Lucknow, the new capital of Avadh, as Asaf-Ud-Daula, son of Shiraj-Ud-Daulah succeeded as Nawabvazir in 1775 A.D. Faizabad went into the hands of Shiraj-Ud-Daulah's widow Bahu-Begum. Asaf-Ud-Daulha's Prime Minister was Tiket Rai Srivastava, who re-established Hanuman Garhi in Ayodhya.

In 1855 A.D. a serious conflict broke out between the Vairagis and Muslims at the site of Hanuman Garhi at Ayodhya, both claiming it to be a place of worship connected with their respective religious King. Wazid Ali Shah's Committee decided the issue in favour of the Vairagis. Faizabad remained completely independent till the end of January, 1858 A.D. By the end of this year (1858) the entire district submitted to the superior military recourse of the British Army.

Modern History of Ayodhya

Modern history of Ayodhya begins with the Sakadwipi Kings who reigned till the abolishment rule in 1955 A.D. which brought the dissolution of the Raja of Ayodhya.

As regards Sakadwipi Kings, the history runs as follows. In the beginning of the 19th century one Mr. Sada Sukh

Pathak was appointed as the Chaudhary of Ayodhya by the King of Delhi. But when Nawab Mirkasim of Bengal became the ruler of the area, his Jamindari was taken away and he along with his son Gopal Ram went to Amroha in the District of Basti, where they settled down in Nandnagar.

Gopal Ram's son Purandar Ram married the daughter of one Ganga Ram Mishir and was blessed with five sons, named Bakhatawar Singh, Shivadhin Singh, Darshan Singh, Iksha Singh and Devi Prasad Singh. All of them became famous in one way or other. Bakhtawar Singh entered the army of East India Company and while his platoon was in Lucknow, the Nawab of Avadh, Sa-a-dul-ali Khan appointed him as the Chief of his force. When once he saved the Nawab's life from an enemy while he was taking stroll, Nawab became too glad and he gave him the Jagir of Baliya. After some time, Nawab Gazi-u-ddin Haider gave him the title of Raja in 1821 A.D. He brought his younger-brother Darshan Singh who too became an officer in the military. After five years, Darshan Singh was appointed Chief of the areas of Sultanpur and Baharaich and came to be known as Bahadur in 1899 V.S. He, also became the area officer of Gonda, and bore the title of Raja. He died in V.S. 1901 (1844 A.D.) at Ayodhya. Raja Darshan Singh built the Shi, a temple of Darshaneshwar Nath and the cement Ghat around Suryu Kund and estate of Darshan-Nagar.

Raja Man Singh was born on the 10th December, 1820. In 1844 at the age of 24, after the death of his father Darshan Singh, he took the lead. He attacked and conquered the fort of Surajpur. The King of Delhi conferred on him the title of Raja Bahadur. Later the title of Kayam-Jung was awarded to him. When Raja Bakhtawar Singh died, he became the ruler of the whole area including Ayodhya. In his period Hindu-Muslim riots at Hanuman Garhi took place. He acted firmly to quieten them.

In V.S. 1913 (1856 A.D.) the Muslim rule ended at Lucknow

and Nawab Wazid-Ali Shah, was sent to Calcutta. The local Avadh people rebelled against the British. During this rebellion, Man Singh saved many English women and children and hence in 1859 A.D. he was given the title of Maharaja at Lucknow Darbar along with a sum of Rs. 7,000. He was one of the most important Talukdars of this region and was also given the title of K.C.S.I. He died in 1870 A.D. at the age of 50. At about the same time his two brothers also died. Raja Man Singh had only one daughter who born a son, Pratap Narayan Singh.

Man Singh wrote the will in favour of his second wife and she in 1875 selected one man named Triloki Nath Singh as his successor. Pratap Narayan submitted petition against him in the court and in 1880 A.D. the court gave his interior judgement in favour of Pratap Narayan Singh who became the King of Mahadauna. Although the suit in the court continued, the British Government conferred on Pratap Narayan Singh the title of Maharaja in 1887 A.D.

In 1890 A.D. the name of Mahadauna Raj was changed to Ayodhya Raj. In 1895 A.D. he was bestowed with the title of K.C.S.I. and later on given the title of Mahamahopadhyaya in 1896 A.D. He was also a member of Legislative Council for two years.

Raja Pratap Narayan Singh was born Asharh V.S. 1912. He married twice and as King of Ayodhya, built Shiva temple of Raja-Rajeshwar. He was fond of making buildings and after he got the title of Ayodhya-Naresh, he made his main centre at Ayodhya and constructed Raj Sadan and its inner residential buildings. He led a simple and religious life and was a very learned man. He was also known as Dadua-Maharaj. He died on the 9th November, 1906 (A.D.).

Pratap Narayan Singh's Will dated July 17, 1891 A.D. made Rani Jagdambika Devi as his successor. In accordance with the Will she adopted the present Raja Jagdambika Pratap

Narayan Singh who is a descendent of Iksha Singh and made him her successor on February 12, 1909 (A.D.). Most of the pilgrims visiting Ayodhya, also pays reverence to this Royal family. The popular belief is that the present Brahmin king is the descendent of Vasistha family with whom the ancient kings of Ayodhya were connected, "The Vasistha were their hereditory priests. The earliest Vasistha was the famous priest of Ayodhya in the reigns of Trayyarjuna, Satyavrate-Trisanku and Harischandra. The next great Vasistha was the priest of Ayodhya at the time of Harishchandra's successor Bahu, who was driven from his throne by the Haihaija-Talajanghas aided by the Sakas, Kambojas, Yavanas, Paradas and Pahalwan form the north-west but Vasistha maintained his position. Mitra Saha Kalmaspado Sudasa, king of Ayodhya had the fourth noted Vasistha as his priest. The fifth was priest of Dilip II Khatbahan and the sixth was priest to Dasratha and his son Rama". (Law: 1954, 21).

Gandhiji came to Faizabad and Ayodhya in 1920 A.D. for his passive resistance movement. In 1939 A.D. a provincial conference was held in Ayodhya under the Presidentship of Late Pandit Jawaharlal Nehru. Thousands of peasants attended this conference and a Khadi exhibition was organised on that occasion.

The Faizabad Gazetteer shows that in the past three big famine troubled Ayodhya. First in 1884 A.D. due to delay of Autumn rains, then in 1877 A.D. and the third in 1907 A.D. which caused much havoc to the area.

Ayodhya at Present: The Holiest among the holy places, the present Ayodhya is situated at 26°27' North Latitude and 82°45' East Longitude on the right bank of river Ghaghra commonly called Saryu river. It is at distance of eight kilometres from its district/municipal headquarters at Faizabad. It is 196 kms. on west of Mugalsarai and 126 kms. from Lucknow. The town has a small but clean Railway station on its West, on the Northern Railway. There is a net-work of roads which are well connected internally and externally with other Cities. Special mention can be made of the National High Way No. 28 which passes through the town. The British following their 1857 A.D. military struggle, began to develop a network of roads here. As there were very few difficult and unsafe roads to travel over the Saryu river there is a long permanent bridge in Ayodhya which links it with Lucknow and Gorakhpur. It is 3,354' long and 24' wide span and fitted with electric lamp posts, on both sides.

To-day, Ayodhya town covers an area of 12.16 square miles or 31.50 square kilometres. The 1961 A.D. census report records its total population to be 17,297-10,776 males and 6,521 females. About 30 per cent of both were literate. A steady increase of population of 26,170 we registered between 1921 A.D. and 1961 A.D. due to influx of people from rural to urban areas and immigrants from the East and West Pakistan and in 1981 the population increased to 30,468. On the basis of religion roughly there are 70 per cent Hindus, 20 per cent Muslims, 5 per cent Jaines and 5 per cent Sikhs. Among Hindus there are about 18 per cent Schedule Castes of the total Hindu population. Being a religious centre and tradition-bound, we come across divisions within one caste also e.g. Ayodhya has a types of Brahmins i.e. Saryupari, Maithil, Kanyakubja, Shakadwipi, Sarnarai Gaur and Oriya. A striking typical feature about Ayodhya is that 80 per cent of its population comprise of Sadhus. The native language of Ayodhya is Avadhi, although people of different caste living there speak their own respective dialect.

In 1920 A.D.—there were two wards in Municipality Section of Ayodhya, but now there are four such wards, namely the Nayaghat, Ramkot, Raiganj and Shringharhat. The town has all institutions of an urban centre under Faizabad Municipality. Out of 25 members of Municipality, 8 members belong to Ayodhya. In 1951 census, 57 names of Mahallas were recognised from the four wards i.e. Raiganj in the South,

Sringarhat in North Central, Ramkot West Central and Nayaghat in the North-West of Ayodhya town.

Ayodhya also has almost all the important institutions of a civilised town. It has several educational institutions, three colleges, sixteen junior High schools and about twenty Sanskrit Pathashalas besides four public libraries. Ayodhya has a long history of learning and culture. The Vedic system of education spread to Ayodhya during the later Vedic period. In the Valmiki's Ramayana Ayodhya appears as a noted seat of learning, known for Vedic schools of the Taitariyas, Kathakars, and Manavars. Among the Brahmins in the town there was neither illiteracy nor inadequacy of knowledge. Asvaghosha (1-2 Century A.D.), Srilabha and Vasubandhu (both 5th century A.D.) were the most celebrated Buddhist Philosophers and authors known to have been associated with the Ayodhya area. Down to 7th and 8th century A.D., both Vedic and Buddhist Systems of education were prevalent here. The only institution of higher learning, according to the modern system i.e. the Saket Mahavidyalaya was started in 1951 as Ayodhya has been a prominent seat of Sanskrit scholarship. In 1956-57 A.D. there were 27 Sanskrit Pathashalas and now the number has risen to 30. The oldest institution called Brahma-Vedic Adarsh Mahavidyalaya at Saryubagh, is said to be founded in 1869 A.D. by Guru Charan Lal Upadhyaya. Teachings in done here in Vedanata, and Darshan Shastra. The other notable institutions are Raj Gopal Sanskrit Mahavidyalaya established in 1882 A.D. by Sri Gopal Das. The Nishulka Gurukul Mahavidyalaya was founded in 1925 A.D. by Swami Yoganandjee.

Now five libraries including the one temple library at Lakshman Kila established by great scholar Yuglananya Sharanji are functioning. Another library at Rajbhawan (Ayodhya Naresh Palace) was founded in 1893 by one Commissioner Colonel not presently functioning and some of its books have been donated to Saket Mahavidyalaya library.

The third library called Ram Granthagar founded in 1944 A.D. by Ram Kumar Dasji has about 10,000 books. The fourth one is really a public library with a Vachanalaya founded by public effort—Bhagvadacharya Smarak Sadan, Sringarhat established in 1972 A.D. Then there is also one temple library under construction under the propoundership of Mahanta of Mani Ram Ji Ki Chhawani named Valmiki Ramayan Bhawan—since four years. One library of Tulsi Chaura is functioning under the supervision of Sri Girivardasji. Besides there are seven printing presses, one cinema hall which has previously Ayodhya Naresh's Auditorium, three banks, 7 small but important factories. However, I must say some thing about Medical and Public Health services. In Ayodhya, as in the past the death rate continues to be high due to influx by aged pilgrims. During Melas a medical officer is stationed at Ayodhya, and compulsory anti-Cholera inoculation is enforced e.g. during Savan Jhula and Chaitra Ramanavami fairs, 77 inoculation posts are set up where pilgrims are inoculated before they are allowed to enter Mela area. At such times all the wells in Ayodhya and on the road sides are thoroughly disinfected This is done by the Municipality. There are five hospitals with a number of private dispensaries which take care of pilgrims and civilians.

Rama-Janmabhoomi and Integrational Movement of Ascetics

(1980-1992) Years old Ramajanmabhoomi controversy took a new turn on the first February 1986, when Mr. K.M. Pandey, Faizabad District judge ordered the district administration to open immediately the two locked gates at Ramajanmabhoomi, which were closed in 1949 following a little suit between the Mahanths and Maulavis. This judgement was highly hailed by ascetics of Ayodhya in particular and Hindu masses in general. Every day from down till dark men and women walked through bylancs of a Ayodhya to catch the glimpse of the silver idols. They came from far and near chanting hymns. Before entering the main temple they kneel to kiss the old marbles threshold of the birth place of the Lord Rama. But next day a group of few Muslim lawyers filled writ petition at Lucknow Bench of Allahabad High Court, challenging the order of Mr. Pandey. The officials of Sree Ramajanmabhoomi Muktiyajna—Samittee approached to the Govt. of U.P. for the liberation of the temple but the Govt. turned down their demands. This resulted into a mass movement and the Mukti Samittee started membership drive to enroll ten lacs members of Hindu community. To seek public support, this committee decided to take out Ramajanaki-Rath from Sitamarhi in Bihar to Lucknow in U.P. for the liberation of Ramajanmabhoomi temple. The committee gave ultimatum to the Govt. of U.P. that if the government is failed to take any decision about the liberation of the place till December, Ist, the patrons of the committee would decide on the further course of action, including. Satyagraha to get it's demand met. Ramajanki-Rath was taken out from Sitamarhi in Bihar on 25th September 1986, supported by Hindu's 'enmasse' and reached Ayodhya on October, 6th. On October 7th several thousand devotees of Rama took pledge 'enmasse' on the bank of holi river Saryu for the liberation of Ramajanmabhoomi and other religious places in U.P. The ascetics of Ayodhya once again took lead and received the Ratha at eastern outer skirt of Ayodhya. The prominent among them were Paramhansa Ramchandra Das and Mahanth Nritya Gopal Das of Digambara Akhara and Mani Ram Ki Chhawani of Ayodhya, respectively.

On 14th October 1986, a huge religious congregation was held at Lucknow to urge the centre and Uttar Pradesh Government to take effective measure for handing over the Ramajanmabhoomi to Hindu representatives without any further delay. As per estimation of Times of India, News service, this was attended by nearly three lacks people. This congregation was presided over by Jagadguru Ramanandacharya-Anant Vibhusit-Shiv Ramacharya and attended by a large number of Dharmacharya, heads of several religious institutions and organisations, Mahanths and saints drawn from different parts of India. Those, who addressed it, appealed to the administration to realise the sentiments of crores of Hindus all over the country and ensured that the place should be handed over to Hindu without any loss of time.

On the 5th April 1987, during Ram Navami festival at Ayodhya, Ramajanmabhoomi liberation movement accelerated, when an estimated 1.5 lacks people took a pledge on the bank of river Saryu that they would neither accept the partition nor conversion of temple into a national monument. Amidts blowing of conchshells and bungles, the seathing mass of humanity gathered on the ghats close to the ancient temples in Ayodhya passed the resolution declaring in unequivocal terms that any attempt by the Government to appease the Babri Masjid Action Committee would invite the wrath of the majority community. If Hindus cannot protect birthplace of their Lord in their own homeland they have no business to exist, the resolution said. Janak Singh of T.O.I. reported, "this was the biggest ever rally organised so far by the Viswa Hindu Parishad especially with regards to disputed shrine at Ayodhya. The rally was presided over by Shankaracharya Sri Swami Vishnudevananda and attended by Mahanth Avaidhyanand of the Gorakhpur temple besides hundred of Sadhus of Ayodhya. An announcement was made in this rally that a trust headed by Ramanandacharya would be formed to built a temple of Lord Rama."

Arousal of public sentiment on this issue was maintained by Vishwa Hindu Parisad on all India level through organising conferences, public meetings for a period of nearly 3 years. In October 1990, they invited 'Karsevakas' from all over the country for construction of Rama temple. The date fixed for the purpose was 30th October 1990. The then Govt. of Uttar Pradesh opposing the move placed entire Ayodhya under Police Cordon. Though the entry into city was banned, thousands of 'Karsevakas' reached Ayodhya breaking the Policy cordon. They were given shelter and food in different ascetic organisations and temples. Mani Ram Das Ki Chhawani and Digamber Akhara become the main concentration point of 'Karsevakas'. The Chhawani was raided by police 3 times and nearly 300 Sadhus and 'Karsevakas' were arrested. On this day i.e. 30th Oct. 1990, morally exaulted 'Karsevakas' moved from Mani Ram-Ki Chhawani in the shape of a procession and reached near Digamber Akhara on their way to Ramajanmabhoomi sthal were joined by Paramhans Ramchandra Das of Digamber Akhara along with many Sadhus and 'Karsevakas'. This process further headed towards the disputed shrine, suddenly police opened fire killing uncountable number of Sadhus and 'Karsevakas'. Those who escaped, reached to the shrine captering it for few moments and caused little damage to the present structure, which was under heavy Policy protection. Here again, they were assaulted by police force. Many 'Karsevakas' and Sadhus lost their lives. The eye witnesses Confirms that probably Ayodhya never witnessed such mass killing throughout it's history.

This incident incited Hindu sentiment throughout the country creating instable political atmosphere. Bhartiya Janata Party, one of the supporting party of central rule withdrew it's support. The then Government of Centre as well as at state fallen down. Hence, entire nation went under poll for seek fresh mandate. Ayodhya and the disputed shrine become the main issue of national politics. One of the political party, Bhartiya Janta Party included the issue in their election manifesto and captured the sentiments of majority community through 'Ramaratha Yatra'. In 1991 parliamentary election, the Bhartiya Janta Party emerged as second largest party in the country. The disputed issue continued as burning issue till the disputed structure was raised to grounds on 6th December 1992 by thousands of 'Karsevakas' led by Ascetics and political leaders.

The above survey of last decade present before us a new integrational and social Activist movement among ascetics of different sects. The 'Sanyasin' and 'Vairagis' who were one time at cut throat competition joined hands on the issue of Ramajanmabhoomi at Ayodhya. The Shankaracharya-head of Sanyasins and the Ramanandacharya—the Vairagi chief, addresed the mass from a common platform. Eminent ascetics like Mahantha Ramchandra Paramhansa, Mahantha Nritya Gopalas, Mahantha Avaidyanath were the leading figures of the movement. This way the ascetics—the guardians of 'Sanatan Dharma' once again assumed their previous role. They mobilised Hindus' 'enmasse'. Ayodhya once again emerged as main centre of attraction for people of majority.

3

ASCETICISM AND ASCETICS: ORIGIN AND DEVELOPMENT

Asceticism is a very developed form of Hinduism. The Hindu Law is divided into four Asramas, the reference of which is available even in the oldest Dharmsutras with slight modification in their names and the serials. Like, Apastamba Dharmsutra places Garhasthya in the first position, Gautam places Brahmacharya first. Vasistha has given the names of Brahmachari, Grihastha, Vanprastha and Parivrajak. The use of the Yati in his Dharmsutra refers to the man of the fourth Ashram of Parivrajak. According to Manu: the fourth Ashram is the Ashram of Yati and Sanyasies. This clarifies that the fourth Ashram had different names like Parivrajak, Bhikshu, Muni and Yati. These words signify the peculiarities of the man in the fourth Ashram. Manu says that the first part of the human life is Brahmacharya, in which he acquires knowledge residing with his Guru. In the second part he becomes a Grihastha after marriage and clears the Pitririna or Devarina. Then seeing his white hairs and loose skin he becomes Vanprastha and spends the third part of his life in forests. The rest, he spends like a Sanyasi keeping aloof from the worldly affairs.

The word Ashram is not found in the Samhitas and the Brahmins but this does not mean that the above four-fold division was not known in the vedic period. The word Vaikhanas of Tandya Mahabrahmin is taken as a synonym of

Vanprastha. If this is taken as correct reference directly or indirectly of the third part of life, is also found in the vedic period. There is no mention of Yati as the fourth Ashram in the vedic literature and the same word found in the different Samhitas and Brahmins is an indicator of a particular caste - Non-Aryan and Anti-Indra. Description of Muni with dirty clothes is found in the Rigveda where Indra is called a friend of the Muni, Muni is called a friend of God in one place. This is thus clear that even in the time of Rigveda there were people who led poor life, lived in Meditation and had lean and thin physique they were called Munis. Probably such people among the non-Aryans were called Yatis. But there is no sense of the Ashrams in these two words. The reference related to Ashram is probably found for the first time in Harishchandro Pakhyan of Aitariya Brahmin.

"Kimnu Malam Kimajinam Ki Musmashruni Kim Tapah".... Here the word Ajin refers to Brahmacharya, Samshu to Vanprastha, Mala to Grihastha and Tapah to Sanyas.

In 'Chhandogyopanishad' it is told that religion had three branches of which the second was Tapah or penance the sign of both the Vanprastha and Parivrajak. Probably there was no difference between Vanprastha and Sanyas upto the time of said upanishad. The word Sanyas occurs in Mundakopanishad and Jabalopanishad. These reference make it clear to that Asceticism was an ancient complex of Indo-Aryan-Culture and the word Muni regularly meant some kind of Ascetic. In later times the word was used as a name for Ascetic because of meditation—Mananat Munih.

While the Varna principle was for the society, the principle of Ashram was for the individual. The Ashrama principle explained the spiritual goal of the individual, guided him now to lead his life and what arrangements he had to make for attaining the highest goal. The Ashram principle was no doubt a very beautiful idea. Three diversified opinions are available about the four Ashramas. Manu is the staunch supporter of the gradual acceptance of the four Ashramas. Overlapping was not admissible. Jabalopanishad established alternatives and allows to become a Parivrajak either after Brahmacharya or after Grihastha.

Gautam and Baudhayan hold that the Grihasthashram only is the real Ashram.

All the above three Ashrams have the vedic support and any one of them can be practised. The word Ashram is derived from the root Shram means a stage of life in which one labours very hard.

It is clear from the directions given by Yagyavalkya to Maitrayee in the Brihadaranyak Upanishad that during those days the Parivrajak had to give up their entire property, wife and other worldly things to lead a begging life. Rules for Sanyas in detail are given in the different Upanishads namely Paramhansa, Brahma, Narad Parivrajak but these are not beyond doubt and as such not to be very much relied upon. For the Yati or Sanyas—Dharma, Gautam, Apastamba, Baudhayan and Vashista Dharmsutras, Manu, Yagyavalkya Smrities, Shanti and other Parva of Mahabharat, Kurma and Agni Puran etc. should be carefully studied.

The attributes of long hair and yellow garments are given in the Rigveda (10/136/2) as typical of ascetics in the full-fledged system of Asceticism. The word Vatarashan occurs in the Rigveda and the same expression in the Taitariya-Aranyak shows that the Vatarasans sages were Shramans and Urdhwamanthins. In the same Aranyak, Prajapati is declared to have practised penance and performed a kind of self-sacrifice. From Prajapati's flesh arose three 'Rishis—Arunas, Ketus and Vatarashanas. From his nails arose Vaikhanasas and from his hair Valkhilyas. Vaikhanasas and Valkhilyas are well known as different kinds of ascetics. In the Rigvedic times there were people who went about naked or downed yellow and soil garments and kept long hair, they were called Muni. Even in the Brihadaranyak the terms Shraman and Tapas occur. Sayan explains these words Shraman to mean Parivrajak i.e. ascetic who has entered into the fourth of the four regular ashramas and Tapas to stand for Vanprastha.

In latter Upanishads, where the Ashram theory is given, the term Shraman is conspicuous by its absence. After Buddha it came to be monopolished by Buddhists. The other qualification of Vatarasan is Urdwamanthin i.e. Urdwaretas which means that sages refrained from sexual life and kept themselves Chaste. If accepted, it follows that in the Rigvedic times there were not only ascetics who were known as Muni but also others who went about naked, exhibiting their great Yogic attainments. A story in the Panchvinsh Brahmin states that Indra restored to life of Vaikhanas who were one class of ascetics. There were Yati also in the Rigveda. If Muni means one who meditates, Yati is one who is controlled. In later literature Yati always means, Person in the last of the four ashramas, a Sanyasi.

R.P. Chanda, however, propounded the view that the Yati were none, but the natives of India following the Indus-valley culture. He affirmed that asceticism and Yogic practices were non-Indo-Aryan in origin. (Chanda, 1920).

D.R. Bhandarkar, considered the Yati as Asur and the Muni as Aryan (Bhandarkar 1940). P.V. Kane observes—"It appears that even in the times of Rigveda, persons who led a pious life of poverty, contemplation and mortification were known and were honoured as Muni, while persons corresponding to them among non-Vedic people were probably called Yati" (Kane, 1930, 53).

A.B. Keith says that Yati in the company of Bhrigu figure in a friendly relation to Indra. (Keith 1925).

G.S. Ghurye, does not find any need to look upon Yati as

of non-Aryan origin. "Yati were also a class of ascetic. Asceticism is a complex of number of traits, the principal one may be distinguished as celibacy, austerity, concentration and ecstacy" (Ghurye 1953).

We know that the Vedic Aryans were fond of Some and with this they describe themselves as having become immortal and having discovered the God (Macdonnel 1897).

The Muni is described as having the Munayonmad i.e. Muni's intoxication (Rigveda—10-136 and 7-56-8) this can be described as his ecstatic trance. Albert Switzer says—"In these hymns we encounter men who know they are uplifted above this world. They are the Shamans and medicinemen—later called Yogins—who get themselves into the state of ecstacy through drinking the intoxicating Soma, through mortification of the flesh and by self-hypnosis...." This consciousness of being uplifted above the world which is experienced in ecstacy is the condition determining Indian world and life negation "(Sanyas)" (Switzer 1936, 22).

It is very significant to find in one of early Upanishad, Taitariya, the supreme soul identified with Ras i.e. juice or flavour. As the Supreme soul is juice or flavour and the drinking of juice produces bliss or ecstacy, so the realisation of supreme soul is attained by blissful ecstacy.

The second element of the escetic complex is austerity, Tapas. Through Tapas asserts a Rigvedic verse, a post can be—hold the old creations of fathers (Keith 1925). In Chhandogyo-Panishad, Yajna is identified with Tapas Mauna i.e. silence and fasting are other kinds of austerity. Panchagni and Trinachiketa are given in Sanskrit literature. Though, in the Upanishads much importance is attached to austerity, yet the Upanishads assert that for the real knower knowledge alone is austerity. The Taitariya-Upanishad says that it was through the practice of austerity that finally came to Bhrigu realise that Brahma was ecstatic bliss.

In the later Maitrayopanishad the practice of austerity is given a fixed and definite place as a stage in the upward spiritual march of the individual mind. Through this mind acquires that Satwa i.e. right attitude which enables to realise the self. But the Brihadaranyak says that without knowing Brahma, the immutable, penance is not fruitful. The Mundakopanishad also subordinates austerity and declares Gyan i.e. knowledge to be superior. In the history of vedic culture Yogic-techniques also came to be formulated and practised. In the Chhandogya Upanishad the great Sanatkumar instructing Narad, identifies Brahma with various mental categories in succession. Dhyan i.e. meditation is the last but one element in the complete Yoga system. In this system Dharma or continued concentration is the final stage. Yoga in its more or less developed form was not only known but was enjoyed and practised as a necessary element in one's spiritual endeavour. Even Hatha-Yoga was well known and its role was appreciated.

Celibacy is another trait of the complex of Asceticism. In general, Asceticism expects and even insists that its aspirants should be taken to it before they settle down after marriage. It is only in the Indian civilisation, which is undoubtedly the mother of Asceticism and Monastic order, that Asceticism is the last stage in an individual's life. Kalidas says in Raghuvansh while describing the customs of the Ikshwaku's that "their stood to the life of a hermit in their old age and in the final stage practised Yoga as a preparation for leaving the material body. "Vardhakaye Munivritinam Yoge Nante Tanutyajam" (Raghuvansh 1-18). This theory is taken to be the ideal since the time Ashrams or the stages of individual's life came to be fixed as four. It is held by many scholars that the fourth stage or Sanyas or Asceticism came to be formulated and recognised fairly late in the history of civilisation. Some scholar look upon the ascetic stage as post-Buddhistic borrowed from the culture that existed in India before the incoming of Aryans, but such views are not acceptable. Not only the separate traits but also the complex or whole of asceticism including celibacy were prevalent quite early in the history of Indian civilisation. The names of the various traits as well as of complex are thoroughly Sanskritic in origin and all other aspects.

The question of celibacy in the Sanyas Ashram has no practical significance. It is significant only when ascetic life is undertaken in Youthful years. Vardhaman Mahabir took to ascetic life without ever becoming a house holder and Buddha renounced the world some times after a son was born to him. He gained knowledge and came to the conclusion that the problem of human life and misery could be solved by renunciation. The ideal type of Buddhistic thought was thus the ascetic, the Bhikshhu. He became the first ascetic—the Bhikshhu and the first founder of the monastic order—Sangh.

The Jabalopanishad declares that one may renounce the world whenever one feels the urge, being imbued with detachment. The earliest and the most scientific renunciation was later known as Naistic-Brahmacharya i.e. confirmed or life long celibacy. A dialogue declares that the Brahmin desires to know Him through sacrifice, through gifts, through austerity of fasting. Having known Him one becomes a Muni, sage, wise one, desiring the same and renounces the world. It means that the Naistic Brahmacharya or Asceticism before marriage was looked upon as the proper course of spiritual endeavour. It is declared that self-realisation brought about by Brahmacharya is not perishable.

Thus, it is clear that first of all sacrifice came to be realised as inadequate for spiritual benefit. Austerity and its allies Yogic practices were thought to be more fruitful. Brahmacharya came to place physical penance as a mode of spiritual endeavour. The need for moral quality of faith and truth was also felt and was given equal weight along with austerity, knowledge and celibacy. Naistic-Brahmacharya, thus, is a fairly ancient institution and is the earliest form of asceticism known and practised.

Some Scholars are of the opinion that the first three Ashrams are ancient and that the fourth Ashram of Sanyas came to be recognised to accommodate the dissenters who had lost faith and sacrifice even before the rise of Buddhism. In the Mundakopanishad final salvation is declared to be achieved by Yati of pure spirit who have cultivated Vedanta knowledge and practised Sanyas. It may be concluded that asceticism or Sanyas had come to be recognised as a necessary step in the endeavour of self-realisation and that it had come to be treated as the fourth and final stage in the orthodox scheme of the individual's life.

It is very significant that Sanaka, Sanandan, Sanatan, Sanatkumar, Sanat-Sujat and Narad are enshrined as immortal celibates who are always ready at hand to give appropriate advice. Suka-Sanak is a combination which is involved to introduce some difficult piece of spiritual knowledge. The Mahabharat and Skandpuran both declare Suka—a celibate. It is, in keeping with the tradition that the Vaishnava sect of Charandasis names itself Suka-Sampradaya. Sanak had so much prestise that the earliest of the Vaishnavas ascetic order of the Nimbarkies looks upon him as its founder. Sananadana figures in Puranas and Sanatan figures in the preceptoral succession as the disciple of Sanaka. Sanat-Sujat figures only in the Mahabharat but in a contact which lifts him up from many ascetics and celebates. Sanatkumar was also a great celibate and he was given the title—Bhagwan. Names of female celebate like Gargi also occur.

The recognition of Sanyas as a regular stage of life or Ashrama itself indicates that not only asceticism was necessary in an individual endeavour but also in that person holding such faith in a group or school. Mokhali or Mankhali was the leader of an ascetic sect called Ajivikas. Rishabha of the Jain's was a King who after some years felt an urge for ascetic life and renounced his Kingdom. The Bhagwat Puran states that he was initiated into asceticism directly as a Paramhansa. If this tradition is accepted than the existence of the Paramhansa order of asceticism goes back to a very ancient date. We may, thus, conclude that at least the four principal orders of ascetics namely Kutichak, Bahudak, Hansa and Paramhansa were in existence even in the time of earliest of the Upanishads. Uddalak, Aruni and Swetkatu were also the greatest Philosophers and were noted as Paramhansa. There was one Aruni who actually combined in his asceticism physical austerity with highest self-realising knowledge.

There are, however, schools and sects of asceticism which have stressed only the physical part of ascetic discipline and raised it to an ideal by itself, either in the form of continuous activities or in the form of more esoteric Hathayoga. The vedic description of Ekvrata as Ishan brings out his peculiarity of physical austerity. He is not connected with any endeavour towards self-realisation so that he represents the earliest practice of physical austerity, more or less as an end in itself. Sarbhanga, and Sutickshna are famous for their austerities. Such ascetics do not figure in the list of Paramhansa in the Jabalopanishad. Besides, Uddalak, Aruni and Swetkatu only Jada-Bharat, Durvashat, Duttatraya appear there in the list of Paramhansas. Use of meat in all conditions of rottenness and even of human flesh, licenced indulgence in sex and such other apparent practices are clearly an anethema to asceticism. Yet ascetic sects indulging in such practices often idealised them as leading to miraculous powers and to final salvation from about the beginning of the Christian era. Such source may be traced in Duttaraya. Strange enough, Duttaraya figures as an incarnation of Vishnu also in more than one list of incarnations. He is the only ascetic incarnation that has now a cult following and a temple devoted to his worship. The origin of Indian asceticism thus seem to be very ancient. With the advent of Mahavira and Buddha there emerged at least two new principles which could not have failed to modify the later developments of asceticism from these origins.

Mahavira and Buddha pondering over the ills of this world concluded that renunciation is the only appropriate part to salvation. Mahavira practised the most austare penance and founded the sect which was called Nirgandha. His younger contemporary Ghosal started his own sect as Ajivakas. The Ajivak sect had both an ascetic section and a house-holder one. Later they appear to have been known as Chhapanakas. The Swetambaras and Digambaras are well known for their organisation. In later history similar situation like that of Siddhartha i.e. remaining on the spot for long apparently in ecstatic trance enjoying His blissful deliverance are described in the lives of Chaitanya and Ramkrishna also. Buddha propounded the view that of One's salvation one has to renounce it. He made five monk disciples and formed a monastic order. Asceticism is ideally the only core and hence the ascetic is the only ideal type recognised by Buddhism. The organisations of these ascetics called Sangha believed in the trio, formed by Buddha, Dharma, and Sangha. Yet this asceticism is more renunciation or rather moderation than self-mortification or austerity. A Buddhist monk was generally known as Bhikshhu, and his female counterpart Bhikshhuni. Jain and Buddhist asceticism laid down duty for an ascetic and that was to preach their respective goal. The Monastic organisation naturally acted as the arbiter in the matter of religious doctrines. This was an element lacking in earlier Indian asceticism. The temples and monastic centres of Hindu ascetics have been discharging the function of serving as an educational institutions not only for ascetic inmates but also for the general public. The Gurukula's, Ashrams of Dhaumya, Kanwa, Valmiki and other were abodes of the vanaprasthas also. The term ascetic itself implies that an ascetic could have had no such establishment. In the Buddhist literature we find the Shramans or ascetics who were followers of perhaps the Jain Digambaras. Sectarian ascetics called Tirthikas, Kumarvratas find their place side-by-side with Dirghajatas.

Ascetics of the most orthodox description were Panchagnitapas. Tridandikas are also mentioned in some lists. It is d ub'ful whether females were ordained into Sanyas although reference to Tapasis are made by Kalidas and Dandi.

The earliest and the first mention of Sectarian ascetics occur in the Maitrai-Upanishad, Athwasiras Upanishad and in Mahabhasya. They were respectively Kapalins, Pasupatas and Shiva-Bhagvatas. In Panchatantra (4th and 5th Century A.D.). We get reference to the settled abode of an ascetic. By that time asceticism had developed into an institution and individual ascetics into the counterparts of Kulapaties, of more ancient data. The abode in which an ascetic resided and received disciples evidently to be initiated into asceticism is called a Mutta, an abode or settlement. In Panchatantra the word 'Mutta' is used an Vidyamutta one of them was not necessarily run by one individual but the others were run by individual ascetics. Once it is mentioned as Muttayatan meaning a monastic centre or convent emphasise the fact of the its being a settled place. To be the owner of the Mutta was to undertake very heavy responsibility. In a Mutta of Ujjain the ascetic was named as Bhairavanand. It shows that the monastic order was older than the Sankaracharya who only renovated the system. The Seventh century A.D. sources mentioning ascetics testify to the wide spread Pasupatas and the Kapalins, and the non-Buddhist places of worship as Deva-Temple. The most important sect of ascetic in northern India in Huient-Siang's time was that of the Pasupatas and the Kapalins ascetic were small in number. There were Nirgranthas also who were mostly in lower Bengal and Orissa. Asceticism retained its Upanishad characteristic to a large extent. The teaching activities of the monastries was in the Upanishadic age, the seat concern of individual ascetic. Dandi refers to an ascetic's named Vamdeo and Maharshi and Bhagwan Marichi. Kapalik ascetics under the designation of Mahavratines are mentioned as residing in the Kapaleshwar temple of Nasik. Existence of Kapalik and Pasupta ascetic sects along sides of Buddhist Bhikshhu is also proved by the drama, Muttavilas-Prahasan written by the Palleva King Mahendra Vikram. Till the end of the 8th century A.D. the ascetic world of India was mainly composed of Buddhist, Jain, Pasupatas and Kapalikas. In Northern India non-denominational ascetics also lived in the ancient tradition of solitary asceticism. It was on such a scene that Shankaracharya appeared in the extreme South-West. He is the counterpart of Sanat-Kumar who lived not less than Sixteen Centuries before him.

No doubt, Vaishnavism of the Vasudeo Cult has already established itself as the Royal Sect, and a number of Gupta Emperors styled themselves Bhagawatas and Param-Bhagawatas. These ISMS at that period did not continue Sanyas, while the Gita insisted on this interested activity as the true spiritual path—the Brahmasutra. It is believed to countenance asceticism. The Yoga system of Philosophy may be said to have encouraged the escetic-trend. Shankaracharya carved out a working compromise between renouncing this world and carrying out one's routined duty. He was himself a Naistic Brahmachari who favoured such disciples. For the consolidation and spread of his religio-philosophical ideas, he established four centres but none of these was selected for basing the monastic centres. The emergencies of temple-colleges meant for house-holders or for ascetics or for both in the beginning of Tenth Century must be attributed to the impetus given by Shankaracharya's organisational activity. In South Kalmukhas are also mentioned who established Muttas and temples in Mysore region. But they disappeared completely from that region after 1410 A.D.

In Southern India one after another Vaishnava teachers and others began a serious campaign against Shankaracharya's doctrines at least from the later part of the Tenth Century A.D. This does not, however, mean that there were no ascetic of importance in Northern India at that period. Huient-Siang observes that there were learned ascetics in Northern India who preferred to teach and write by themselves and declined Royal-Patronage. Four about a century after Vigyaneshwar, who wrote his Mittakshara, we have no knowledge of any great ascetic excepting Gorakhnath, who founded the sect of Kanfatta-Yogins and helped in giving a final death blow to Buddhism especially in Northern-Eastern India. Prominent heads of Gorakhanathis are known as Peer which shows that Gorakhanathis comprise in some may with the Muslims.

For the next great ascetic we have again to turn to the South finding Ramanujacharya who took to asceticism after his marriage. He is said to have founded the Vaishnava school of asceticism known as Tridandi. The heads of religious centres founded by him or belonging to his religious school are however, not ascetics. At the same time the devotional songs and other literature of the Alwars at South were strengthening the Vaishnava devotion. Nimbark, the life-long celibate founded the ascetic sect known as Sanak-Sampradaya or Sundershan-Sampradaya which is the oldest among the existing Vaishnava sect.

Ghurye propounds that in actuality the honour of being the first to found organised Vaishnava asceticism belongs to him though Raṃanuj is believed to have introduced Tridandi asceticism among Vaishnavas. This sect substituted Krishna and Radha in place of Vishnu and Lakshmi. The next great ascetic Madhwacharya was an ascetic of the Shankara School but broke away from it. He elaborated his own system of devotion centering it around Lakshmi Narayan. Other ascetics were Vithalpant whose son was Gyaneshwar. Precepter of Gyaneshwar was his elder brother Nebritinath, was the disciple of a Nathpanthi ascetic. Vishnuswami was the promulgator of the fourth Vaishnava sect which had Radha-Krishna as its tuitiliary diety. Ramananda, who was ordained into asceticism as Vaishnava Vairagi installed Rama as Personal God and tuitiliary diety. To his subject goes that credit and the honour of having the largest ascetic membership and the biggest contingent of the Militant Ascetics. Thereafter one great ascetic Vidyaranya also appeared. Asceticism registered a definits departure from the strict theory of ascetic life in the lives of Vaishnava Ramananda and the Shaivite Vidyatirtha. Both of them considered their duty to defend Hinduism against he onslaughts of Islam. This marks a new departure in Indian asceticism. A little more than a century, after Ramananda there is an evidence of a politically important ascetic of Mewar but his name is not known. Manasudan Saraswati of the Sixteenth Century A.D. was ordained into asceticism by Vishweshwar Saraswati and he plays the cause of Vaishnavite devotion centered round Krishna. Eknath of Maharashtra bears testimony to the ascetic of that part. The devotion of Tulsidas centered round Ram is a wellknown fact. Ramdas of the Seventeenth Century A.D. forms the next land-mark in Indian asceticism. He was a follower of Madhwa sect of Vishnavism. He founded 14 monastic centres in Maharashtra to defend Hinduism against Islam. He started a new sect in Maharashtra and cultivated the school of Ram worship. Thus asceticism may be said to have come to age and to have got ready to step forward to undertake active social work. (Ghurye 1953).

4

VAISHNAVISM: ORIGIN AND SPREAD

The several systems of Indian thought do not appear immediately after the close of Vedic period, they do so considerably later, although the exact duration of the intervals cannot be determined. Indian thought made rapid strides in this interval, which was one of the great intellectual stir not only in this country but also elsewhere as in *Greece*. New and very important School of Religion and Philosophy also definitely emerged then. Among several ISMS, Vaishnavism is the Creed in which Vishnu is worshipped as the Supreme God. Vishnu is also a vedic deity. He is represented in the hymns as one of the solar deities and as such, is associated with light and life. This essential feature, as depicted in the hymns, is his taking three strides, which probably refers to the rising, culmination and setting of the sun. It was this worship of the sun, the swift moving luminary, that gradually transformed itself into the worship of Vishnu as the Supreme God. The word Vishnu means Vishnoti-Jagat, that pervades the entire world and it is formed with the root Vishnri in the sense of pervading. Vishnu had already attained supremacy in the time of the Brahmins and also in one of the older Upanishads. The goal of human life is represented as reaching the Supreme abode of Vishnu—Tat Vishnoh Paramam Padam (Kathopanishad—1/3/9). And allied conception was of Narayan, whose origin may be traced in Rigveda and which appears in a well developed form in the Brahmins. The name signifies the abode or resting place of men or, more generally, the goal of all beings. One of the Brahmins states that Narayan placed himself in all the world and all the Gods were all placed in Him. In the Mahanarayan Upanishad, Vishnu occupies the position which Shiva does in the Shiweteshwar Upanishad—Tutakimchit Jagat Yasmin Drisyate Sruyatepiva Anter Bahisca Tat Sarvam Yvapya Narayanah Sthitah. He is called in the epic the son of Dharma. It employs that the conception is not merely cosmic but also pre-eminently ethical in its character. A third element as prevalent in this period also goes to form Vaishnavism but it is derived from a non-vedic though not a non-Aryan source. They seems to have arisen in the North-West of India a religious reformer Shrikrishna, the son of Basudeva, who preached Atheistic faith. The Supreme God termed as Bhagwan (the worshipful) was a God equally exalted morally and otherwise. It soon assumed a sectarian complex in the form of Bhagwat religion. This creed in course of time came to be combined with the Vedic cult of Vishnu-Narayan and it was this combination that chiefly contributed to make the God of Vaishnavism even more personal than that of Shaivism. Somewhat later Srikrishna was deified and identified with Vishnu-Narayan as a incarnation of Him.

Thus, altogether three streams of thought mingle to form Vaishnavism. Vaishnavism also contains elements from sources other than the Vedas. The form of the Supreme worship which the Vaishnavism comments, is for the most part based on the Agamas. Among the special features of this creed the few are given below:

(i) The Vaishnavism is more rigorously monotheistic than Shaivism.

(ii) Vishnu assumes different forms or incarnation called Avatara (Keshavadhrit Budh Shareer) etc.

The word Avatara signifies that God brings himself down,

in order to present to us a higher ideal of life—

Yada Yada Hi Dharmasya
Glanir Shavati Bharata
Abhyuthan Dharmasya, Tadatmanam Srijamyaham
Paritranaya Sadhunam
Vinasaya Ch Dushkritam
Dharm Samsthapanarthaya, Sambhawami Yuge-Yuge
(Gita—IV-17 and 8)

This theory of Avatara helps Hinduism in its absorptions of other creeds into itself by explaining the God's worshipped in them as but manifestation of the one supreme being (Gita 9/23). Thus, it does not exterprate those creeds but re-interprate them and utilises whatever elements of truth they may contain. Thus, the worship of Srikrishna himself was assimilated, to Vaishnava creed and that still later a place was found for Buddha also among the ten principal incarnations of Vishnu.

(iii) Vaishnavism lays great emphasis on loving devotion (Bhakti). Like Shaivism, Vaishnavism also holds that Vishnu is knowable through loving devotion.

(iv) The Vaishnava religion discarded animal sacrifices evincing thereby its antagonism to the conspicuous feature of Vedic religion.

A special mark of monotheistic belief, whether Shaivism or Vaishnavism has the distinction it makes between God, the individual soul and the world. The soul is usually conceived as eternal but as entirely dependent upon God. Therefore, it becomes the first duty of man to make himself a conscious and willing instrument in the fulfilment of his purpose. Generally speaking mone-theistic belief wanted to reach the presence of God or become God like. The main means of achieving this and is, besides good conduct (Charya), loving devotion to God (Bhakti) which will gain his grace (Prasad).

Vaishnavism and Shaivism were both in a flourishing condition and each of them had six principles of division. The Vaishnavas embraced those who are termed Bhaktas, Bhagawatas, Vaikhanasas, and Karmhinas. Each of these sects was sub-divided into a practical and speculative portion. This Karma and Gyan sub-division formed twelve classes of the Followers of Vishnu who believe him as a soul and supreme deity. The Bhaktas worshipped Vishnu as Vasudeo, they were no characteristic mark. The Bhagwatas worshipped him as Bhagwat. Their persons were impressed with the usual Vaishnava signs representing the discuss (Chakra), Club (Gada) etc. They also paid reverence to the Saligram-Shila and Tulsi plant. They, on many points approach to the present point of Ramanuja although they cannot be regarded as the same. The Bhagwat is one who follows particularly the authority of the Bhagwat-Puran. The Vaishnavas worships Vishnu as Narayan with the usual marks on their persons. They promise themselves as a sort of sensual paradise. The Shaktas of the Vaishnava class, worshipping the female personification of Vishnu and observing the ritual of the Panchratra are called Chakrins or Panchratrakas. The Vaikha-Nasas appear to have been, but little different from Vaishnavas specially so called. They worship Narayan as Supreme God and wore his mark. The Karamhinas abstained from all ritual observances and profess to know Vishnu as the soul source of some of the Universe. The Vaishnava forms of the Hindu faith are still sufficiently numerous. The great divisions of Ramanuja and Ramananda are un-noticed.

"In this religious country of India Vishnu is being worshipped from the Vedic period but during the Vedic period Vishnu has not attained so much importance. The worship of Vishnu became prominent during the Mahabharat period end the Narayaniya religion of that time is called Bhagwat-Dharma—Complete surrender has its great importance in the Bhagwat-Dharma (Upadhyaya, 1953). Vishnu worship became very elaborate these days. Though in the Vedic period Vishnu also was among the deities but had no place of importance rather He was a deity of fourth grade. He was called Trivikram Uruvikram and Urugaya and this mention of three strides gives the conclusion that the name Vishnu was given to the Solar-God. Only, five or six hymns of Rigveda are in praise of Vishnu but in Aitariya-Brahmin Vishnu is described as the Supreme God. This shows that gradually at the Brahmin period the Vishnu worship was attaining importance. During the Upanishad period Vishnu got a place in Trimurties. Historically, we may say that at least a thousand years B.C. Vishnu attained a prominent place in the Hindu deities. Loving devotion also got importance and prominence gradually with the increase of religious worship. The famous Sloka of Gita (18/66) Sarva Dharma Parityajya clearly indicate the value of Prappati. Vishnu worship was very popular at the time of Panini also. At the time of Mahabharat, Vishnu was worshipped in the shape of Krishna and Narayan.

The Vedic ideas preached that the entire schemes was placed under the law of Karma i.e. to say that every individual shall reap the fruit of deeds he or she performs in previous lives. But a new doctrine that the operation of this law can be modified by the grace (Prasad) of the God combined with the loving faith i.e. Bhakti. The worship was preached among others by the Bhagwatas or Pancharatras. They tought Bhakti for Krishna, identified with Vishnu-Narayan. Rival sects like Pasupatas and Suras threatened to destroy the solidarity of the Aryan community which was however checked by the doctrine that Vishnu is identical with Shiva. This compromise prepared the ground for the doctrine of Trimurties.

The age long epics have eventually imbibed into themselves the Aryan and Non-Aryan elements of mythology and have created a sound back-ground for the Hindu religion which has remained almost the same in the following centuries. Along with the Vedic element, the epics presents three sectarian

Gods—Vishnu-Krishna, Brahma and Rudra-Shiva. The worship of Brahma as creator i.e. Sristikarya is an outcome of Upanishad period. The authors of the epics exaults the position of Vishnu-Krishna by incorporating the characters of Narayan and Vishnu-Krishna in the Vedic Vishnu and by Brahminishing the cult of Krishna who was the war Lord of the Abhiraj. In the Harivansh, Krishna appears as the Supreme Vishnu born on the earth. Karmarkar observes that "While Srivishnu arose out of religious notions and beliefs of the Non-Aryan and Aryans, Vaishnavism emerged as a combination of many faiths found in the Brahmanical and non-Brahmanical circles. To avoid the sectarian rivalry a notion of Hari-Har also came into being." (Karmarkar, 1949).

The Rigveda, the Satpath Brahmin, the Kathopanishad, the Taitariya and other works show the different stages through which Vishnu was attaining eminence. In the Bhima-Parva of Mahabharat the supreme spirit is addressed as Narayan and Vishnu, and identified with Vasudeo. The Anu-Gita speaks of the Virat form shown by Krishna to Utank as the Vaishnava form. The Mahabharat brings about parity between Vishnu and Shiva. The notion of the Awataras appears to have just made beginning in the epic period. Both, Krishna-Vasudeo and Rama are identical with Vishnu and thus they are Gods on the earth. The Taitariya Aranyak for the first time speaks of Narayan as the Supreme being. The Mahabharat identifies Vasudeo-Krishna with Narayan who bears that name because of his resting place in water. The Bhagwat-Gita describes Vasudeo to be all. The personality of the Supreme Krishna appears to have resulted from the fusion of the Brahmanic tradition of Brahma Vishnu and others and the Bratya tradition which added its doctrine of monothism and Narayan.

The Vaishnavism preached in the Mahabharat is varied in Character. Vaishnava elements in the epics are mainly found in the Gita (6-25-42), the Mokshadharma-Parva (12-

174-367) and the Annu-Gita (14-16-51). At some places Vaishnavism is depicted as Pantheism to which is super-added a personal God, at others it is a theistic doctrine explained away by the Vyuhas. The doctrine of the Vyuhas set forth in the Narayaniya section may be summarised as follows:

(i)	Vasudeo	—	The Supreme Soul, the internal ruler of all.
(ii)	Shankarshan	—	Primival matter, prakrity.
(iii)	Pradyumna	—	Cosmic mind, Manas.
(iv)	Aniruddha	—	Cosmic self-consciousness, Ahankar.

It is said that sometimes one Vyuh is tought and sometimes two, three and four.

Akantic religion, equivalent also to Narayaniya, Shatwata, Bhagwata, Pancharatra or Vaishnava however, is stated at many places to be the best form of Vaishnavism. The Narayaniya (12-334-51) is the earliest exposition of the Akantic-Dharma which preaches sole devotion to Narayan or the Supreme Lord as the only means of seeing Him. The system is said to be originally promulgated by the Seven Rishis (Saptarshikul). The Chitra-Shikhandines, the Shantiparva states that this Dharma was revealed to Janmajay in the Hari-Gita and also that it was narrated to Arjuna at the beginning of war.

Suvira Jaiswal states that "Under the Patronage of Guptas, Vaishnavism reached the climax of its popularity. The fact that Sri Lakshmi, the Goddess of Wealth and plenty was united with Vishnu during this period bears testimony to the growing prestige of the new religion, which spread from one of the country to another and extended to the Indian Colonies of South-East-Asia. It enjoyed full support of the rich nobility and traders, merchants, and priests, as shown by its followers, women, agriculturists and craftsman as indicated by archaeological and literary sources. The religion kept its door open to all the four Varnas, and, with the prestige and authority it derived from the support of higher classes, it must have influenced deeply the masses also, and was apparently responsible for preserving the Varna System and reconciling the masses to their social and economic conditions" (Jaiswal 1967, p. 216).

This way Vaishnavism is one of the most important religio-philosophical sect of India. There are at least four important philosophical view points among the Vaishnava-ascetics as the name Chattum Sampradaya prevalent among them. Though the underlying unity is provided on the theological plane by the recognition of some form of Vishnu yet in daily worship his different aspects create significant differences. The followers of Ramanuj worship Vishnu in the aspect lying on Shesha and attended by Srimbhu and Lila. He is fundamentally different from Sita-Ram the tuitillary deity of the followers of Ramananda. Ramananda and his followers, however, are in point of philosophy the followers of Ramanuj. On the other hand tuitillary deity of Nimbarkies, Vishnuswamis and Vallabhacharies is Krishna with Radha. The Madhya-Gaudhwavites, generally worship any form of Vishnu as well as the combination of five deities Panchdeo.

The Vairagies are marked off from the Sanyasis by their white garments. They are not clean Shavan but some of them keep the hair matted like the Sanyasis. Their Tilak mark distinguishes them from the Sanyasi. The material for the same and shape and design too are different.

Vaishnava Asceticism is probably later than the Shaiva-Asceticism. The Ascetic schools before Shankaracharya were probably all Shaivites. Hazra, however, shows that "some texts in Mahabharat and a passage in Kautilya's Arthashastra employ Vaishnava Ascetic. It is not known that Ramanuj founded on ascetic sect. His predecessors had names ending with Muni shows that they were ascetics. There were before them, in the Tamil land Vaishnava devotees who were known as Alwars, who have been placed sometimes before the fifth or Sixth Century A.D. The names of the earliest three Alwars end in Yogin but it cannot be ascertained whether all the twelve Alwars were ascetics" (Hazra, 1940). G.S. Ghurye concludes that on the whole Vaishnava Asceticism as a regular practice cannot be dated earlier than the Ninth Century A.D. (Ghurye 1953).

Ramanuja is the earliest Acharya among the four Sampradaya of Vaishnavas. But not many of the Ramanujee Ascetics are known. Nimbark, has been looked upon as a contemporary of Jaideo, the author of Gita-Govinda. He is only the historical founder of Nimbarki-Sect and the traditional founder is God-Vishnu himself incarnate as Hamsa. Sanaka and Sanatan the traditional eteral celebate were the disciples of Hamsa-Vishnu. Therefore, the sect is also called Sanakadik or Sanatan or Sudarshan. Nimbark brought Radha with Krishna to the forefront as the tuitillary deity. Radha in this cult is treated as the wife of Krishna and not as mistress. Like other Vaishnavas Vairagi, Nimbarkis put on white garments, their names end in Das or Sharan and their Tilak mark consists of two white vertical lines with black dot in the centre. Their necklace rosary consists of two strands of Tulsiplant which lies close to the neck. The ascetics of this sect great one another with Jaisarveshwar Dandwat. The nimbarkies are grouped into nine Dwaras each one named after its founder a noted ascetic of the sect. Almost all Vaishnava sects accept that the Vishnuswamis were not at the outset designed for ascetic. Vishnuswami himself as an ascetic started his ascetic sect Rudra-Sampradaya. In this sect there are four Dwaras.

Vallabhacharya (1479-1531 A.D.) turned an ascetic sect almost completely into one of house-holders. Madhwacharya belonged in origin to the Shankar school of Philosophical Thought but carried on a ceaseless campaign against that school. His sect is known as Brahma-Sampradaya and its tuitillary deity is Lakshmi-Narayan. Two of his immediate successors were Tirthas—a class of ascetic not possible in strict Vaishnava sect. Chaitanyas, though only one, of the branches of Madhwa—they themselves as Gaudiya and Radhavallabhies, are by far the largest and most important group. Their house-holder section, which is quite large, acknowledges its Madhwa—affiliation by calling its members Madhwa-Gaudeshwaras. The Radhavallabhies, who are the small sects are divided. Their Rasik section which is mainly composed of house-holder, looks itself as independent Chaitanya is treated as incarnation, not only, of Krishna but Radha and Krishna combined. They are having more than a dozen of sections. The Madhwa-Gaudiya looks upon Radha as Krishna's Mistress and not as his wife. The sect formally does not recognise cast. They were their Tulsi necklace quite close to the neck unlike Madhwas, who wear it rather loose. It consists of three strands. Most of the Vaishnava ascetics and a large number of Gaudiya Mission are wearing Ochre coloured cloths. Their Tilak marks consists of two white perpendicular lines joined over the bridge of the nose from which another white line continues down the bridge of the nose to its tip. They called themselves Tridandi-Sanyasi and name of male ascetics end in Das or Sharan and those of female in Dasee, though staunch Vaishnava, they also observe Shivaratri fast.

The most important Vaishnava sect is that of "The Ramanandis, who are, otherwise called Ramawat. Though they do not like to be grouped with Ramanujees, their philosophical basis qualified dualism is acknowledged to be that of Sri Sampradaya—the first and the oldest of Vaishnava Sampradaya. At the very early age Ramanand got himself initiated into Sanyas at the hands of Raghawananda. According to Ramanandies their school begins with Ram and the doctrine descends through Sita and their devotee Hanuman through a succession of twenty-two preceptors to Haryanand.

R.G. Bhandarkar (Bhandarkar 1913) states that "Ramananda had separated and founded a district school during the life time of his preceptor. Ramananda made it a regular practice to accept disciples irrespective of their caste affiliation. His one of the famous disciples was a woman named Padmavati. Among his Sudra disciples twelve become very famous. The different branches are called Dwaras as stated in the foregoing pages."

Ayodhya, being the main centre of Ramanandies has seventy-one ascetic organisations commonly known as Mutta-Sthan. The organisation Badasthan and Vidyakund are believed to be the oldest among all. Badasthan came into existence not earlier than second quarter of Eighteenth Century but it is very important centre. It was founded by one Ram Prasad Dasjee who took to Sanyas after marriage and gave Janki-Bhasya to the sect. He also started a new style of Tilak known as Bindushree. The Bindu, mark of red lead in the middle of two white lines, representing Sita's forehead mark. This centre has the largest number of followers. At Ayodhya itself Baba Maniram Dasjee Kichhavani commonly known as Chhoti Chhawani headed by Mahanth Nritya Gopal Dasjee is under the same spiritual lineage. Another old important centre at Ayodhya is known as Vidyakund having affiliation with Rasik-Sampradaya.

With the advent of Swami Agradasjee of Raiwasa Gaddi, Jaipur in the year 1632 V.S. a new esoteric Sadhana-Padhati was developed among the Ramanandies and was called Rasikopasana. This Gaddi become the principal seat for this cult. In the Sampradaya's literature this has five synonyms like Janki Sampradaya, Rahasya Sampradaya, Rasik-Sampradaya, Jankivallabh Sampradaya and Siya Sampradaya. Out of these five, the name Rasik-Sampradaya caught popularity among the followers. The founder of this cult Swami Agradasjee uses to call the followers Rasik. The Rasik are those devotees of Lord Ram who meditate on the deity's personal inter-course with his wife. They consider themselves one of the bossom girl friends of Sita-Ram who takes part in the sexual-intercourse (imaginative) between the God and Goddess. At present, Ayodhya, the centre of ascetics with Dasya, thinking have been pervaded by the Sadhus of Rasik Sampradaya. Kanak-Bhawan, Ayodhya is the principal seat. The Dwara started by Swami Anubhawanandjee. The Baddi-Chhawani of Raghunath Dasjee, another big centre of Ramanandi ascetics is affiliated with it. Ascetics owing allegiance to Baddi-Chhawani are spread far and wide. The Ramanandies have their centres spread over in other places than Ayodhya also.

Among remarkable personalities of the Ramanandies at Ayodhya are—Swami Nritya Gopal, Dasjee, the youngest Mahanth of Baba Mani Ram Dasjee Ki Chhawani, engaged himself in social work and also constructing a huge Valmiki Research Centre and Valmiki Mandir.

Sri Paramhans Ramchandra Dasjee of Digamber Akhara deserve special mention who is actively engaged in social development and political activities. He is associated with Bharat Sadhu Samaj and is also the Ward Commissioner in Faizabad Municipality. Baba Pagaldas, Master of Music is running a School of Music specially of Mridang Vadan and attracting the Music lovers, not only, from India but from U.S.A. and other countries of West.

Mahanth Mangal Das is another renowned personality of the sect holding Sanskrit school and is famous for his scholarship. Kailadhish Sita Ram Sharan of Lakshman Kila, one of the present leaders of Rasik Sampradaya is gaining popularity for his oratory and Sanskrit teaching. In his credit there are many books in Sanskrit. He also publishes a monthly paper named Saket carrying valuable articles and news about Sampradaya and Bhakti systems.

Among Ramanujites—Swami Jagadguru Ramanujacharya-Purushotamacharya of Sugrivatila is an ascetic with devotion to social spiritual upliftment of mass. He is leading an *Akhand Jyoti* representation of spiritual awakening. He is also running a school for Sanskrit Vedanta. All the above personalities of Vaishnava Sampradaya are working with devotion, for spread of Vaishnavism. They have been able to attract a good number of Chelas from Western countries. It is known to every one that Krishna Bhakti cult is flourishing in United Kingdom with its centre in London. These organisations are popularly known as Hare-Krishna Society founded by a Vaishnava Ascetic from South India. Thus we can say that Vaishnavism has crossed the boundaries of nations and is in the process of Universalisation.

5

ASCETIC LIFE—DIKSHA TO SAKETVAS

Ascetic life starts from Diksha i.e. initiation into the cult by Guru, Classical Indian Texts have attached much importance to Diksha (initiation). While explaining its importance, it is said that initiation is compulsory for an ascetic because no religious ritual bear any fruit if a man is not initiated by Guru. It has been elaborately explained that even a minor good action of an initiated person gives fruitful results, while great religious rituals even become fruitless of an uninitiated one. Therefore, initiation is essential for getting Sadagati after death "God is the almighty and He is creator of entire Universe and His abode is therefrom where nobody return if one reaches there" (B. Harit Smritti 1-16). The greatest religion is to be the Das of the Lord Hari (Ibid 1-18).

It is absolutely necessary to always have the idea of being Das of Vishnu because, those who are not the Das of Narayan are the living Chandals (B. Harit Smriti 1-120). Only properly initiated person is entitled to be the Das. For ascetic life, initiation is like birth into the fold of asceticism. A Novite is being initiated into the Vaishnava cult as per the process described in foregoing pages. After initiation, symbol of the cult works as identity mark. Vaishnavism makes the most use of symbols. In all its scheme of teaching and practice it seeks to make definite approach to the reality by suggestive type of symbol—an approach that can never find its goal, but can only draw nearer and nearer as it points successively like the ancient Greek Philosophers to the symbols or likeness which most fully and faithfully reflects the true, and embodies the largest part of reality which in its entirely is inconceivable by the human mind and inexpressible in the language of men. The symbol is the necessary and helpful intermediary, between the inadequate capacity of mind of the would be worshipper and the incommunicable nature and the fullness of the unknown whom he addresses. The uses, purpose and types of Vaishnava symbols as prevalent among the ascetics of Ayodhya are dealt with in this Chapter, with symbols and different sectorial marks of Tilak as observed during field work.

Vaishnava ascetics of Ayodhya have a typical vegetarian food habit and they adorn themselves with typical dress suitable to the ascetics.

Various roles performed by ascetics as religious specialists, Mahanth, priest, devotional singer and musician and transmitter of knowledge have been discussed in this Chapter. The Chapter ends with the description Saketvas which is the last performance and end of ascetic life. This way, we can say that ascetic life starts with initiation and passing through different stages and ends with Saketvas.

Process of Initiation

There are five stages or Samskaras of initiation prevalent among the Vaishnava ascetics of Ayodhya and these are described in the Bridh Harit Smriti also.

1. Tap Samskar

The first of the Samskaras is the acceptance of the Chakra (disc) etc.

First of all a pious Vaishnava Mahanth or Brahmin is to be approached who is pure, truthful and possesses the knowledge of the necessary performances and Mantras and is well versed in Vedas and Vedangas, who is associated with a pious Sampradaya and with Gyan and Bairagya, and such a Guru will examine the Shishya for at least one year. If he is a good character and is a devotee and keen in the service of the Guru and if the disciple (Shishya) is found fit, his five Samskaras will be performed strictly according to the rule.

Having taken bath early in the morning and after worshipping the God Vishnu in a pious place, the disciple will approach the Guru for the worship of the disc or Chakra etc. with Panchamrit and Panchgavya. Before the God Vishnu, the same will be worshipped with the necessary mantras with flowers, Dhup, Deep and various Naivedyas. With the Purussukta oblation will be given to fire with Ghee and Kheer. The obligations will be also given with the Gayatri Mantra. Thereafter the five emblems of Vishnu or two emblems of Ram (bow and arrow), as the case may be, will be put-in fire. Then again oblation will be given with Chandakchhar Mantra, and the Shishya will go round the Hom Kund. Then he will, after Namaskaaras to God Vishnu or Ram and perform Jap. Then Acharya reciting Mantras will put the marks on the body of the Shishya seated with concentration seeing towards the east. The mark of disc or Chakra will be put on the right arm, that of Sankh or counch on the left arm, of Gada or club on the middle of the Bhal, of Nandak on heart and the pure Sarang mark will be put on the Mastak. The last three i.e. Gada, Nandak and Sarang marks are not in the practice these days. After this the marks will be washed by water and worship will be performed again. The Vaishnavas will be given a feast. The belief behind this is that these performances wash away all the vice. This Samskara is the best Samskaras of Vaishnava because it is accepted that one attains the greatest achievement by this Tap Samskara. A Vaishnava ascetic without mark is to be discarded from all the works because he is sure be go to hell. Then the next Samskara is Pundra Samskara.

2. *Pundra Samskara*

Worshipping Lord Vishnu or Ram, the Shishya should worship the Guru also, get his Pradachina done, and according to instructions of the Guru he should accept Pundra with great devotion with pure white clay. Because without the Tilak mark all religious rights, Swadhyaya and Dan etc. became, fruitless. Without the Tilak mark on the forehead if a Vaishnava ascetic feeds others on the occasion of Guru Parva he goes to the Raxhas (Damons) and only Mal-Mutra goes to him for whom the feast was performed. The Vaishnavas should be careful to have Urdwa Pundra. Only and to keep aloof from the Triak Pundra (of Shivites). The mark should begin at the origin of the nose and should go up to the end of forehead. It should be taken on Lalat (forehead), Bhuja (arm), Chhati (chest) and on Udara (stomach) also. It is their belief that God Vishnu in the shape of different names like Keshava, Madhava, Madhusudan etc. reside in the different parts of the body.

3. *Kanthi or Mala Samskara*

According to the rules prescribed, the Guru offers Kanthi of Tulsi beads and directs to keep the same as required according to the rules of the Sampradaya and always to show respect and have full faith in the same. They wear it also in their necklaces. A Vaishnava without Kanthi is not respectable.

4. *Nam Samskara*

This is performed on an auspicious day. After taking bath Lord Vishnu and the Guru are to be worshipped with flowers and other materials.

The name of Das should be given after the name of God governing the particular month in which initiation is given. Vaishnava name is given only or to a Dixhit as a non-Vaishnava name is totally forbidden Jap and Homa are also performed and Vaishnavas are to be fed on this occasion.

5. *Mantra Samskara*

After this, Mantra Samskara is necessary. Early in the morning one should take his bath and worship God. The Guru is also required to do the Jap of the Mantra Ratna. He is then required to ask the disciple to come in Pure Clothes with a Kalas (pitcher) full of water. The Kalash should have the five auspicious Palava (leavees), Patra and Managal Dravya. The disciple is to be blessed with Vishnu Suktas and then 'Homa' is to be performed with Purus Sukta and Sri Sukta. The Acharya is required to remember his own preceptor and his Guru Parampara and God and pray to them. The disciple is to approach the Guru very respectfully and humbly and request him for the Mantra. According to rule the Guru is to perform Mantra Samskara after which Dakhina is to be offered by the Shishya.

With the these five Samskaras a disciple becomes a Dixhit and comes under the Guru Parampara of his particular Vaishnava Sampradaya.

The above-mentioned procedure of initiation are based on Sastric (Textual) prescribed form which is at present being strictly observed by the Ramanujitee. Among the Ramanandi Virakta, Whose numbers are more at Ayodhya and most of them are not well read, the process has been simplified. In place of Vishnu's mark they use Ramayudh i.e. bow and arrow. The existing system, as observed at Ayodhya, is as follows:

At the time of initiation the person to be initiated as Virakta takes bath and gets his head shaved leaving some hairs at the top known as Shikha. Then he approaches the Mahanth, Guru with all materials for worship. The Guru puts Tilak mark on his forehead and presents Tulsi Garland. Thereafter the subject sits in Padmasan, and the Guru after covering his head with a cloth, recites Kharashar Mantra in his right ear thrice. Afterwards the disciple offers salutation known as Dandwat and worships the Guru with offerings and then takes Charnamrit i.e. water by which the feet of Guru have been washed. From that a very time he thinks that he has become one with Sita-Ram. After this he takes four rounds of the temple known as Parikarma and offers his salutation to all the senior ascetics. During night hours he offers his services to the Guru where he is being taught the esoteric process of worship i.e. Sadhana Padhati. Then they are provided with new clothes and they put off the old for ever. During the service period to Guru he is given a new name Das. He is put under trial for Six months, and his activities are being observed by the ascetics. After confirmation about his good conduct and character he is provided with Langot, the symbol of keeping Brahmacharya (austerity) which includes the following materials:

(i) Safee: Cloth to cover the head
(ii) Langot: Two pairs of cloth pieces
(iii) Achala: One cloth to cover the 'Langot'
(iv) Kamandal: Pot to carry water.

During this period he is taught to follow the following rules strictly:

(i) To observe fast on 11th day of both the fortnights known as Ekadasi.
(ii) At the time of nature-call he sits keeping his face towards the sun and covering the head with cloth. After that he must wash the anus with soil.
(iii) To wash his left hand three times and the right hand two times and both the hands two times with soil.
(iv) To wash the water pot three times.
(v) To throw the water from his mouth in the left side only.
(vi) To finish his bath reciting Ram Nam.
(vii) To offer Arghya to sun.

(viii) To recite Ram-Raksha-Stotra.
(ix) To sit on Asan and to do Jap at least 108 times.
(x) To worship the Lord Rama and the Guru.
(xi) To spend his time in Bhajan and Swadhyaya.

The Ramanandis always wear the Tulsi rosary whereas the Ramanujee wear it only on auspicious occasions. The Ramanandis are of the opinion that without Tulsi rosary i.e. Kanthi there is the danger of impurity and attacks of evil thoughts and spirits.

Urdhwapundra: The Forehead Mark of Vaishnavites

Urdhwapundra is the Vaisnava sectorial mark commonly called Tilak. It is the most important symbol of Vaisnavism. Since Rigvedic times, we find that the cult of meditation has sprung along with the cult of fire sacrifice. Hinduism makes the most use of symbols and Vaisnavism shares a larger part. To understand the depth of religious emotion underlying the form of worship, it is essential to know the symbology of ritual. The symbol is the necessary and helpful intermediary, between the in-adequate capacity of mind of the would be worshipper and the incommunicable nature and fullness of the unknown whom he address. The Vaisnava contentions that the symbol is a signpost and a guide to better higher thoughts and a true worship of Him, whom no form can express or language describe.

The symbol serve the purpose of providing in material and suitable form a convenient object of reverence, to meet the spiritual need of those whose minds through darkness and ignorance are unable to grasp the conception of an unseen, formless deity. It also sets forth invisible or audible likeness that cannot be really or fully expressed to the physical eye or ear, or even clearly conceived by the limited faculties of the human mind, (Geden 1909: 141).

The ascetics were or are the emanatist of all religions.

They have propounded religious philosophies and symbols to guide the people in their spiritual endeavour. The founder of any ascetic cult and their followers live devout lives according to their religious convictions which they express through the variety of symbols. All the Tilak observed by author posses wonderful mythology as well as spiritual and philosophical interpretations, and also works as dynamic entity within its context of action in Vaisnava asceticism.

It has special importance among Vaisnava ascetics. This is a principal part of sectorial code of conduct. Among the ascetics of Ramanand Sect, secret of worship only taught to the disciple of the same sect wearing same 'Tilak'.

The Vaisnava asceticism at present has four major sects named after it's propounders. These are Sri Ramanuj (sri) Sri Nimhark (Sanakadi or Hamsa), Sri Madhwa (Brahma) Sri Vishnuswami (Sri Ballabh or Rudra). These are commonly called 'Chatuh-Sampradaya'. Sri Ramanujacharya popularised Vaisnavism in Eleventh Century A.D. His sect is commonly called Sri Sampradaya. After his demise in the year 1137 A.D., the spread of Vaisnavism was continued by his successors. The most prominent among them were Sri Lokacharya and Sri Vedant Desik (13th cent. A.D.). The first gave preference to Tamil Texts and the second accepted the authority of Sanskrit Tradition. It is why the followers of Lokacharya are called Tenkalai, who maintain that the female energy of the God head, though devine, is still a finite creature that serves only as a mediator or minister (Paruskara) to introduce the soul into the presence of deity. They also maintain the responsibility of devine grace and utterhelplessness of the soul till it is seized and carried off like a kitten by it's mother before the danger that threatened it and this doctrine is called 'Marjat-Kishore-Nyaya'. The 'Vadakalai' insist on the concumittancy of human will in the none of salvation, and represent the soul that lays hold of God as a young monkey who grasps it's mother in order to convey to a place of safety. This is called Markat-Kishore-Nyaya'. (Crook 1909: 87). Variations of above theories brought about variations in the mode of making the 'Urdhwapundra'. The 'Vadakalai' make a parabolic form, the base of which is nearly in a line with brows. It is like letter 'U' and called 'Vadagal' (Fig. 4.2) The 'Tengkalai' use a somewhat straight mark, slanting in opposite directions outward and supported on base, which is itself a small triangle, base upwards with the vertex lowerdown about the apex, or in some cases, the centre of the nose. It is like letter 'Y' and called "Tingal" (Fig. 4.1). The centre streak in the middle is common to both. Both the two straight lines and the bottom connector are made with white clay (Gopichandan), and the centre streak is made with turmeric powder of red colour. In both the above cases, the two white lines represent Vishnu's feet, whilst the red line in the centre is made in honour of Sri or Lakshmi, the consort of Vishnu. Ramanand, an ascetic disciple of Raghwanand of Ramanuj order introduced 'Ramavat' cult replacing Vishnu and Lakshmi, the truitilliary deity of Ramanuj by 'Sita and Rama'. The worship of Rama and Sita introduced by Ramanand in early 15th cent. A.D. caught popularity in Northern India. His followers and probably the largest, with their Chief Monastries at Ayodhya and Benaras. He himself used the 'Tingal' mark of Ramanuj. His followers explained the two white lines as representative of Rama and his brother Lakshman, the red streak in the middle made in the honour of Sita. Further more they recognised the triangle at bottom as throne of the deity (Singhasan), which also represent Hanuman (the monkey God). Some scholars of the Vaisnava sect levels two more interpretations of Urdhwapundra. One group believes that two vertical white lines represent Gyan (knowledge) and Vairag (renunciation), the middle red streak or dot symbolises-Bhakti (devotion). Another group opines that two vertical white lines symbolises Brahma (God) and Jeeva (soul), the middle line represents Maya (illusion). These two interpretations seem to be intellectual stir only.

Types of Vaisnava Secterial Marks

The ascetics of Ramanand or Ramavat Sampradaya do not disclose the internal secret of worship to a person of other Sampradaya unless and until he accepts their Tilak mark. Sectoral secret of worship is only taught to the disciple of the same sect, wearing the same Tilak mark. This is strictly followed by the ascetics of Rahasyopasana or Sringar Cult of Ramanandies, commonly known as Rasik Sampradaya. At present, there are nineteen types of Tilak (Urdhwapundra) prevalent among the followers of different Acharya Gaddies (Teacher's seat) belongs to Chatuh Sampradaya-Vaishnaya at Ayodhya. They are as follows:

1. *Laskaree or Vijaishree* (Fig. 4.3)

White Tingal Urdhwapundra with white middle line. Founder of this Tilak was Swami Balanand of Jaipur.

It goes to say that in ancient days, the followers of Ramanand, while offering Sandhya, were once attacked by the Sanyasis, the followers of Shankara. In that utter confusion they could not find time to put the red mark in the middle, and as advised by Guru Balanandjee they put on only three white lines on their foreheads and engaged themselves in battle achieving victory over Sanyasis. From that day they continued to wear the three white lines on their foreheads, and named it Laskaree or Vijaishree. Ascetics of Baddi Chhawani and Vidyakund of Ayodhya are of same order.

The two renowned disciples of Baba Raghunath Dasjee of Baddi Chhawani brought a little change in the Tilak mark.

(a) Swami Mauni Ram Sharan Dasjee put a word 'राम' at the base of inner white line (Fig. 4.6).

(b) Swami Ram Udardasjee put two words 'राम' and 'सीता' each side of the middle line (Fig. 4.7).

2. *Bendi Tilak* (Fig. 4.6)

White Tingal Urdhwapundra and one white round mark

in the middle. This Tilak was founded by Swami Ram Prasadacharya of Badasthan Ayodhya.

Once Swami Ram Prasadacharya forgot to put red Sri mark in the middle and went to sleep. In the morning he was surprised to see the mark of red Bendi. He came out with the same and was objected by the ascetics of Sampradaya for change in Tilak mark. Then he tried his maximum to remove it but of no use, it remained present on his forehead. Then Acharya drew a conclusion that it may be given by mother Janki, the wife of Lord Rama. From that very day the Acharya and his followers started putting the same mark on their forehead. Ascetics of Badasthan and Chhoti-Chhawani are the followers of same order. After a lapse of time ascetics of this order started putting the mark in three different sizes: (a) Rupaya Bhar: One rupee coin's size, (b) Athani Bhar: 50 paise coin's size, (c) Chawani Bhar: 25 paise coin's size.

***3. Chatturbhujee Tilak* (Fig. 4.5)**

White Tingal Urdhwapundra with upper portion turned at 90° angle in opposite direction. No "Sri" mark in the middle. Founder of this Tilak was Swami Narayan Dasjee of Bihar.

Once at the time of a Bhandara, organised by Narayanjee, while he was attending the Panghat, his Langot fell down from the back, when his attention was drawn to the same by a person sitting in Panghat, he replied that his hands are busy and it is for Narayan (Lord Vishnu) to set the 'Langot' right. Astonishingly, two more hands joined the body of the Saint, corrected the langot and vanished away. From that very day the Saint made this mark on his forehead and called it Chaturbhujee i.e. four armed. The ascetics of Swargadwar of Ayodhya out the same mark.

The above three Tilak marks contain some mystical power of their founders, whereas the other types described as follows are on the basis of their esoteric Upasana called Rahasyopasna. The different Acharyas of this sect started putting different kinds of Tilak with their own explanation. All these Tilaks are called Sri Tilak. They are as follows:

1. *Sri Tilak of Rewasa Gaddi or Agradasjee Ka Tilak* (Fig. 4.9)

Vadgal, white Urdhwapundra, red Sri in the middle and two Chandrika (half moon mark) at both side, of yellow colour (Fig. 4.9). Founder of this tilak was Swami Agradasjee of Rewasa Gaddi, Jaipur. Swamijee is considered as the founder of Rahasyopasna in the Ramanandi Sampradaya. In this Upasana, the devotees assume themselves as a female who is among the near Sakhis or friend of Jankijee. They worship the Lilarup of Lord Rama, attended by many females. Ascetics of Tapasijeeki Chhawani, Ayodhya are of this order.

2. *Ramcharan Das Tilak* (Fig. 4.16)

Vadgal, Yellow, Urdhwapundra with Yellow round Sri Bendi and Yellow Chandrika just above bendi. Founder of this tilak was Sri Ramcharan Das, a disciple of Swami Ramprasadacharya of Badasthan, Ayodhya. When he went to learn Rahasyopasana at Rewasa Gaddi, he was asked to change the Tilak. Then he preferred to change it. The Acharya of the Gadi asked him to change from Tingal to Vadagal with Yellow colour. From that very time, the followers of Ramcharan Das use to put this mark. This way the Bendi Tilak of Badasthan was separated as Sringari Bendi. Ascetics of Janki Ghat, Ayodhya are the followers of the same Tilak.

3. *Srijiwaram Ka Tilak* (Fig. 4.11)

Vadgal, Yellow Urdhwapundra with Yellow Bendi and Yellow Chandrika just above the Bendi, on both side painted Mundrika (Ring) with Sita Ram. Founder of this tilak was Sri Jeevaramjee of Golaghat, Ayodhya.

Sri Jeevaramjee was previously disciple of Sri Shankar Das of Chiran, Chapra, Bihar, became the Sadhik Chela of Sri Ram Chandra Dasjee. Then after he introduced a new type of Tilak. His followers, settled at two places, one at Chiran,

Chapra and another at Ayodhya. Mahatma Yuglananya Sharanjee, Mahatma Jankivar Sharanjee and Mahatma Ramballabha Sharanjee were the ascetics of highest spiritual merit in this order. In Rasik Sampradaya, this Tilak has the largest number of ascetic followers. At Ayodhya, Golaghat, Lakshmankila and Rinmochanghat are the main centres of this Tilak.

4. *Srijanak Raj Kishori Sharan Rasik Ali Ka Tilak* (Fig. 4.14)

Vadgal white Urdhwapundra with Bendi and Chandrika in the middle of Yellow colour. Founder of this tilak was Sri Janak Raj Kishori Sharanjee, Rasik Ali, Ayodhya.

Sri Rasik Ali is considered as one of the great Acharya of Rashasyopasana. He was the disciple of Mahatma Raghava Das. By the permission of Guru, he became Sadhikchela of Ramcharan Dasjee. The ascetics of Rasik Niwas Ayodhya are his followers. One of his disciple Ram Sewak Sharanjee established his seat at Swargdwar, Ayodhya known as Bavanjee ki Gaddi.

5. *Sri Rupkalajee Ka Tilak* (Fig. 4.13)

Tingal, Yellow Urdhwapundra with red Sri and red Bendi in the middle and just above the Sri, Yellow Chandrika and two Yellow Mundrika at both sides of the Urdhwa Pundra. Founder of this tilak was Sri Rupkalajee of Ayodhya. The name of Rupkalajee was Sitaram Bhagwan Prasadjee but he is famous as Rupkalajee only. He was the disciple of one Mahanth Ramcharan Dasjee of Bihar who was of Tingle white order. But after coming into Srinagar Sadhana he changed the Tilak mark. His followers are in large number from Bihar. Ascetics of Rupkala Kunj, Nayaghat, Ayodhya are the followers of same order. One of his disciple Sri Ram Puja Sharan, popularly known as Divyakalajee, established one Sthan nearby Rupkala Kunj, and named it Divya Kala Kunj at Ayodhya. This is one of the leading Centre of Rasik Sampradaya at present.

6. Rupasarasjee Ka Tilak **(Fig. 4.12)**

Tingal, white Urdhwapundra, Red Chandrika, Red Bendi, Red Sri in the middle.

Founder of this tilak was Rupsarasjee of Ayodhya. He belongs to the Galtagaddi of Jaipur. He established Jaipur Mandir at Ayodhya and introduced this Tilak mark. The present Mahanth Sita Ram Shranjee of Lakshman Kila and ascetics of Charushila kunj are the followers of the Tilak.

7. Ramsakhejee Ka Tilak **(Fig. 4.10).**

Vadgal, yellow, Urdhwapundra with Yellow Bendi in the middle. Founder of this Tilak was Sri Ramasakhejee.

Ramasakhejee introduced a system of worship known as Sakhabhava in Ramanandi Sampradaya. He was the disciple of Madhwa Sampradaya's Gaddi Udupi (south India). He established four Sthans at Ayodhya and introduced the new Tilak. The Ascetics of Nitya-Raghava Kunj, Shravan Kunj, Saryu Mandir and 'Ram Sakhe ki Bagia' are the followers of this Tilak.

8. Kamnendu Mani Ka Tilak **(Fig. 4.8)**

Vadgal, white Urdhwapundra with white Bendi in the middle. Founder of this Tilak was Sri Kamnendu Manijee.

He was only one known person to practice the worship with Suhrid Sakhabhava in Ramanand Sampradaya. Ascetics of this order resides in Saket Raj Bhawan, Ayodhya.

9. Karuna Sindhujee Ka Tilak **(Fig. 4.15)**

Vadagal, white Urdhwapundra, Red Bendi and above it Red Sri in the middle.

Karuna Sindhujee went to Rewasa to learn Rasikopasana and put one Red Bendi in his previous Tilak. The followers of Chandra Kala Kunj Ayodhya are of this group.

***10. Swami Narayan Tilak* (Fig. 4.17)**

Vadgal, Red Urdhwapundra with Red Sri in the middle. Founder of this Tilak was Swami Narayanjee, Chhapiya. He introduced this new Tilak with as explanation that Sri or Shakti or Mother Goddess in the main governing deity and the Jeeva and Brahma both are under her. To show the domain of Mother Goddess the introduced Red Tilak. The followers of Chhapiya Mandir, Ayodhya, belong to this category.

***11. Nimbark Ka Tilak* (Fig. 4.18)**

Nimbarkies are of Vadgal Parampara. They put white Vadgal mark only upto the middle of head without any Sri mark in the middle.

***12. Madhwa Ka Tilak* (Fig. 4.19)**

Madhwhites are also of Vadagal group, but they make the Tilak mark of black colour and called it Shyamsri, without any Sri mark in the middle. The explanation is that the Tilak is representative of Lord Krishna, who was of black colour. So they put black Urdhwapundra only.

These Tilak marks are put on the twelve parts of the body such as middle of the head, forehead, neck, both arms, both fore-arms, chest, both side of body, stomach and shoulder. On going into the above details about Vaisnava Urdhwapundra, one is bound to admire the dexterity of the Vaisnava Gurus that they devised the symbols first to mark the path of asceticism on the individual and secondly to distinguish various sects and sub-sects in Vaisnavism from each other. The symbols also attract the followers towards each other, and the commoner to give alms to an ascetic. Anthropologically speaking, there could not be a better way to show distinction and reverence in a religious order. Mention may be made that the saivite have their own distinct symbol as compared to vaisnavites. But as the latter have numerous sects and subjects based on incarnations of Vishnu and the philosophies of gurus it simplifies the more complex symbolic forms.

Food Habit

As a rule all Vaishnavites are vegetarians and abstain from wine, meat etc. At Ayodhya, the number of Ramanujites are very much less than the Ramanandis. The Ramanujites are not only strict vegetarians, but also observe purity. Nothing must be eaten by a Ramanujee which has not been prepared in a strict privacy and by themselves. No one else is allowed to enter into the kitchen and he himself enters only after taking bath and putting woolen or silken garment on the body. They always use Arwa rice. Pulses like Masoor and Urad are discarded. They neither use spices nor they use prohibited vegetables like onion and garlic. They neither take tea/coffee and also never use sugar in their meal. In place of it they use Gur. They also keep themselves away from taking meal at a Grihastha's house. Before taking meal they offer Bhog to Lord Vishnu and put leaves of Tulsi Plant for purification. They discard intoxicants like Ganja, Bhang etc.

Ramanandis are also strict vegetarians. Their meal is cooked by Bhandari, who should be a Brahmin. In their diet they take only one time meal i.e. lunch. They are not so strict in eating only Arwa rice. They also take their food in Grihastha's places. They can eat Pakki-Food e.g. Puri, Halwa etc. at Dwija's Place, but cooked rice is only at Brahmin's house. The Vairages sits in Panghat at the time of Bhandara or otherwise also for taking meal. Every Ramanandi before taking meal calls Jai of the followings:

> *"Charo Sampradayan Ki Jai, Bawan Dwaron Ki Jai,*
> *Anant Koti Vaishnavon Ki Jai, Apne Guruki Jai,*
> *Hanuman and Garuda Deo Ki Jai, Ramkrishna Deo Ki Jai,*
> *Sri Maha Prasad Ki Jai, Jai-Jai Sita Ram, Jai Radhe-Shyam"*

The Vairages of Akhara are in the habit of taking Bhang

as intoxicant. However, it cannot be denied that there are so-called Sadhus among the Vaishnavas also who indulged in low worldly affairs and in this way are the black spots of the Organisation. They should be deemed as exceptions. The Ramanandi Vairages have their own names of various materials.

Dress

The general Vaishnava ascetics of Ayodhya wear Salmon coloured or white cloths. The Akharies among the Ramanandis wear silken or woollen cloth but the general Vairages put on white cloth. Achala, Coppin, Langot and Chhadar are the only cloths worn by the ascetics. The Ramanandi always put necklace of Tulsi Plant but he Ramanujee only keep it with them and wear on the auspicious occasions. The Khakis among the Ramandis go about naked with only langot of Banana skin. Their body is powdered with dust and ashes and their hairs and nails unclipped. Other Ramanandis like Vairages wear only white clothes. Some of them allow their hair to grow long while others keep themselves as Mundit-Mastak. This system is called Panch-Bhadra and Panch-Keshin. As a foot wear they use Khadan or Chhatti made up of wood only or they walk bare-footed. Some of the Ramanandis also keep a cloth for covering the head which they call Ram Namka Safa. The Ramanujites wear Yagyopavit whereas the Vairages keep themselves without it because they feel Yagyopavit is only for Grihasthasram.

Ascetics as the Religious Specialists

It is well-known that religion plays an important role in the life of Hindus, and as such, people in general and religious minded persons in particular are associated with the religious activities prescribed by the Hindu Shastras and perform Yajna from time to time at different places. Although religion expects human qualities that are meant for the peace and perfection and purification of the individual and the society. Still different functions are also prescribed as the subsidiaries. Vrat, Upavas,

Pujas and Kirtans etc. are prescribed for the awakening of good ideas and ideals, noble thoughts and impressive actions. It is clear, therefore, that the main idea behind the Religious rituals is the purification of life which is absolutely necessary for one's own interest and also for the society and the country.

India, from the centuries before, has always been aiming at the world peace and prosperity and the Vedic Hymns from the Upanishadic thoughts, the Panoramic legends have been always directing Hindus to do good for the self and for the greater self. The ascetics right from the Vedic ages have been discarding the worldly pleasure in order to achieve such a spiritual power which could do the best for them and also for others. Indian culture has been much influenced by the ascetics and their light Vashista and Vishwamitra, Valmiki and Vyas, Bharadwaj and Augustya and other ascetics likewise had attend perfection and had done much for the welfare of the country. Even during the present centuries their tradition has been maintained by sages like Ramanand, Pramhans, and Vivekanand, Dayanand and Aravind etc. by infusing modern out-look to the traditional deep thoughts of the predecessors.

India, a land of holy places, has always attracted saints and Veetrag and in places like Ayodhya, Brindavan, Hrishikesh and Puri sages of esteemed order are still available. The Ahobal Baba of Kashi, Brahmachari Basudewacharya, Nritya Gopal Das, Mangal Das, Pursothamacharya of Ayodhya may be mentioned as the ascetics of that order.

The disciples play an important part in keeping the spiritual tradition alive among the general public by preaching performing, organising religious moods and functions and giving necessary directions to the general public specially belonging to the rural areas and maintaining the same tradition in their own life. Though, the domestic priest was mainly engaged by the public for the performance of religious rites still ascetics also are given importance in this matter.

The ascetic in a large number are at present associated with various Mahanth Gaddies of different holy places and in places of devotion to Ram, Krishna and Vishnu cult. Almost all the temples are managed by those ascetics so far as religious functions are concerned in nearly 424 temples. In almost 75% of the temples ascetics are the Pujaris either of the Ramanuj or of the Ramanand or of the any other Sampradaya. From morning till midnight they are the ascetics who keep themselves engaged in worshipping the deities according to the prescribed rules and also in allowing or disallowing, visitors and guiding them so far as religio-activities are concerned. At Ayodhya they are also the guide for a new comer who wants to pay homage to God Rama and others in different temples and also to know the history of or the legend associated of the different holy places. On the bank of the holy river Saryu even we find the Pandas, Pilgrims feel themselves pleased by getting Darshan of ascetics engaged in meditation, Pujas, Kirtan or Katha Pravachan, who give solace to the people in distress, generally asked them to perform Ramdhun and also show them the ways and means for getting initiation if desired. Of course the present day atmosphere has influenced the ascetics also and it must not be doubted if any such report received that the ascetics of different sub-Sampradayas have tried to drag any disciple to their own camp. But such a case is rare because the present day public are seldom influenced in such a way. Even if persons from rural areas may be influenced in that way such a case occurs rarely because they also are generally guided by their village folk. That is to say, that if an important person of a particular village is a disciple of a particular Gaddi, others also from that village generally approach the same Mahanth of getting Diksha.

It may be mentioned here that most of the ascetic Gaddies of Ayodhya earn a lot from their disciples. The disciples spread over the different parts of India and also abroad offer Dakshinas from time to time to the Mahanth and during the time of special functions like Guru Purnima in the Gaddi special Dakshinas are received from them. The tradition goes so far that the disciples offer Dakshinas on the different happy occasions in their family like, birth, Upanayan, marriage and construction of new building etc. Even at the time of Shradha, Guru Dakshina is offered. Moreover, the Mahanth himself also pays visits to the places of his disciples and receives offers. Whenever any special function or Katha-Pravachan is organised Dakshina comes to the Mahanth and to his associates. Some of the ascetics earn by worshipping or by organising Kathas, Kirtans, Pravachans and also by declaring future happening the ascetics earn their livelihood wholly or partially, by some kind of religious services as they are the religious specialists. It may be noted that at the time of initiation handsome offerings are made to them.

Mahantha

The Mahantha occupy a favourable position as the religious specialist of Ayodhya because they are all associated with different Gaddi having good building and agricultural lands received from the disciples or purchased with the money offered by their devotees. They usually receive offering in cash and kind from their Chelas at Ayodhya and abroad and whenever they go elsewhere they are received with great devotion and handsome Dakshina is received by them. The Mahanths of high order, if they are at the same time good foretellers or impressive Katha-Vachaks, earn a lot.

Priests

The ascetic priest engaged in different temples earn their livelihood by worshipping the deities. They also earn some thing if and when specially offered to them by the visitors. If they are called for Kathas or are engaged in Kirtan, Ramdhun, Ramarcha etc. they get some thing which helps them for their livelihood. Priests who know Astrology also earn in that way.

Devotional Singers and Musicians

At Ayodhya one may come across a few devotional singers and musician ascetics also. They keep themselves engrossed in devotional songs concerning Ram and others and in this way generally earn their livelihood. People, visitors specially are much attracted by them and they offer Dakshina to them. Some interested in music of classical type are also their students. Special mention may be made of one Pagal Das Baba whose deep songs greatly impressed the entire holy city of Ayodhya, and his two disciples were the foreigners from United States of America. They were learning Mridang.

In this way, it has been explained that the ascetics of different orders at Ayodhya are the religious specialists of the holy-place in as much as they earn their livelihood by getting offerings, guiding religious rituals like Ramarchas, Katha-Kirthan, and also with the help of Astrology and devotional songs. It must not be forgotten that some of the ascetics of Ayodhya are the reciter of the Vedic Mantras who also receive handsome offerings from the orthodox Hindus and from the curious foreign visitors. It is curious to note that the present day ascetics of Ayodhya are more or less acting as the Brahmin priests for householders. If the trend continues there is a fare chance that a new Brahminical order will emerge in the shape of Vaishnav ascetics. It is clear from the present study that Vaishnava ascetics are working as the catalist for healthy Grihastha life and are solely dependent on their follower Grihasthas. This way they are working in tune with Society.

Ascetics and Transmission of Knowledge

Ascetics recite sacred Hindu scriptures in different regional languages at different Mutts and by such mediation between Great and Little tradition they provide ground for the interaction between a Great Tradition and a Little Tradition. Thus, these ascetics who recite Katha are the traditional Channels for transmission of knowledge. Not only this they also work as Cultural Media in expansion of Hinduism or Indian Culture to the other countries. They make disciples from every part of the world. Devotees from other places come to know about Hinduism from these ascetics. All the them do not interact equally with these Tirthyathries and similarly they also do not act equally as a traditional media of the transmission of knowledge.

There is a group of ascetics who have specialised themselves in transmitting the knowledge of sacred. They may be called as the backbone of Hinduism. Mathadishas and Katha Vachaks come in this category. Most of them are well known among the Hindus of India and Nepal, e.g. Sita Ram Sharanji-Kailadhish, Ram Narayanacharya Maniparvati, Brahmachariji Smarak Sadan; and Gujarati Baba who Command very high respect among Ayodhya-Vashis in particular, and among Hindus in general. These Katha Vachaks are empowered with the knowledge of Purana and Vedas.

The ascetics, Katha-Vachaks may be classified into three categories:

(a) Who arrange their Katha personally.

(b) Whose Kathas are organised by an individual or a group.

(c) Third type of Kathavachak are those who are invited by the different institutions on festival days and such other occasions.

Generally, it has been observed that a Ramayani or Kathavachak before reciting any sacred texts, explains what is Punya and Paap what a Hindu should do or what not to do; how one should lead social and religious life, to the audience generally from the rural areas, as most of them coming to Ayodhya spent some of their time in listening to Katha. In this way these ascetics play an important role in adding the knowledge of sacred to a pilgrim or local devotee.

Death-Saketvas Performances

The Vaishnava ascetics believe that death is not the end, but to be one with Lord Vishnu at his abode i.e. Saketdham. The general practice among the Vaishnava ascetics of Ayodhya is either to float the dead body in the river or to burry it under the earth. The first one is called Jal-Samadhi and the other Bhu-Samadhi. Only two ascetics centres have reported about Dah-Samskar i.e. burning the dead body and that too also only of Mahanth. Those organisations are: Rajgopalsthan and Karuna Sindhijee Ka Sthan.

The common practice of disposing-off the dead body among the Vaishnava ascetics is as follows:

At first the dead body is kept on a funeral stand known as Viman, made up of bamboo sticks. Then the ascetics carry it on their shoulders upto the bank of a river. There, they put it on the ground and perform Arati with camphores, they garlands the dead body by flowers. The Shishya changes his old cloth by new one, then the dead body is carried by a boat in the middle of the river where they tie up the dead body with sand bags or stone then put it into deep water. Thereafter all the ascetics present, performs Tilanjalee and returns to their places. At their Sthanas they wait outside the gate where Pujari of the Mutt spray Shankha-Jal i.e. sacred water kept in conchshell then only they are allowed to enter in the Muttas. The ascetics of Sthan performs Akhand Kirtan for the departed soul.

On the thirteenth day they arrange for Bhandara i.e. common feast. It is arranged as per the capacity of the Mutt. In Bhandara, there are only three lines: Panghat one only of Mahanths another of general ascetics and the third of the Grihasthas participating in it. These Bhandaras are of two types:

(1) *Pyara Bhandara*

In this type, a limited number of ascetics participate in it.

(2) *Shambhu Vesh Bhandara*

This Bhandara is open to all ascetics / non-ascetics whosoever comes, will get cooked food duly packed up in a new cloth called Gamchha. The expenditure of this type of Bhandara is enormous.

After food, the Mahanths are provided with a Dhoti, Chaddar and a nominal amount of money as a token of regard. Ramanajee's observe Sudrak for ten days like Vaishnava Grihasthas.

In this way, the Ascetic life starts with Diksha and running through different stages, playing different roles ends with Saketvas.

6

ASCETIC ORGANISATIONS OF VAISHNAVA'S AT AYODHYA

In the fourth Chapter, I have discussed the life-cycle of ascetics at Ayodhya. This Chapter deals with the present situations of ascetic organisations, of Vaishnavas as observed during the field investigation at Ayodhya in 1979-80. The Ascetic Organisations (Muttas) at Ayodhya can be classified into three categories:

(1) Vaishnava
(2) Shaiva
(3) Udasin

Again Vaishnava Organisations here can be classified into two major groups.

(a) Ramananda Sampradaya
(b) Ramanuja Sampradaya

The Shaiva cult has only three Organisations at Ayodhya where only six ascetics are residing. The Udasin has two Organisations holding a huge number of followers. But peculiarity is that in Ayodhya they have no dominance neither more than a handful of persons of the faith. The City of Ayodhya is the main centre of Ramanand Sampradaya, may be because Rama, incarnation of Vishnu and tuitillary deity of Ramananda Sampradaya was the king of Ayodhya. The ascetic consider it as a Jagrat-Dham-Saket. The Ramanuj

Sampradaya has only twelve Mutts here, rest of the entire city is pervaded by the Mutts of Ramanand Sampradaya. These ascetic organisations may be discussed at two broad levels.

(1) Textual
(2) Contextual

The present treatise deals mainly with the contextual aspect of ascetics belonging to two principal Sampradaya of Vaishnavas, (1) Ramanujee and (2) Ramanandi. The date collected from seventy-one Vaishnava ascetic organisations are spread in all the four Municipal Wards of Ayodhya/ Faizabad. Their largest concentration is in the Ramkot area and on the bank of Saryu river. The total number of ascetics permanently residing in these organisations comes to 3,000 of which only 12 are females. There are also ascetics who live in individual houses or in caste temples other than the Mutta. Their approximate number will not be more than 200. At the time of important festivals like Ramanavami, Gurupurnima, Janki-Vivah etc. number of the ascetics visiting this City exceeds 12,000. They temporarily accommodate themselves in the Muttas or reside independently on the bank of Saryu river. There is no Mutta of Ramanujee having any female ascetic. All the twelve female ascetics are of Ramananda Sampradaya residing in four Muttas, exclusively for females at Ramghat area. The largest number of ascetics resides permanently in the following three Muttas:

(1) Hanuman Garhi
(2) Chhoti Chhawani
(3) Baddi Chhawani

Seeing the similarities of organisations, their functions, routines etc. Eight Muttas or organisations were selected as a sample for holistic study, six from Ramanand Sampradaya and two from Ramanuj Sampradaya which are discussed in this Chapter.

(A) Ramanand Sampradaya

(a) Chhoti Chhawani
(b) Lakshman Kila
(c) Baddi Chhawani
(d) Hanuman Garhi
(e) Bada Sthan
(f) Ram Ballabha Sharan Kunj.

(B) Ramanuj Sampradaya

(a) Kaushlesh Sadan
(b) Vijay Raghaw Sthan.

The Hanuman Garhi has been discussed in Chapter-VI, alongwith Vaishnava Akhara System and list of all other ascetic Organisations have been given in Appendix. In all the Organisations Mahanth is the Head. He sits on the Gaddi. He initiates candidates into the mysteries of cult, he superintends the worship of idol and the accustomed spiritual rights, he manages the properties of the organisations, he administers its affairs and the whole assets are vested in him as the owner thereof in trust for the institution itself.

Mahanth-ship is not alienable or a partible.

(a) The headship of a Mutt is not a matter of partition.
(b) The property of the Mutt is also not partible.

Mahanth can be removed on the following grounds:

(i) being of unsound mind;
(ii) his sufferings from any physical or mental defect or infirmity which renders him unfit to be a trustee;
(iii) his having ceased to profess the Hindu religion or the Mutt;
(iv) his conviction for an offence involving moral turpitude;

(v) breach by him of any trust created in the respect of any of the properties of the religious institutions;

(vi) waste of the funds or properties of the institution or wrongful application of such funds or properties for the purpose unconnected with the institution;

(vii) adoption of device to convert the income of the institution or of the funds or properties for purposes unconnected with the institution;

(viii) leading an immoral life or otherwise leading a life which is likely to bring the office of the head of the Mutt into contempt;

(ix) persistent and wilful default by him in discharging his duties or performing his functions under the act or any other law.

The above points have been accepted in-toto by the Government of Madras State, while making law for the Hindu religious organisation. The law is known as *Madras Hindu Religious and Charitable Endowment Act 1959.*

Mahanth, as Sarvadhikari of Mutta appoints Pujari, Kothari, Utaradhikari, Bhandari etc. as given in detailed description of each organisations in the following pages. The detailed study of the organisations contains their history, present position, administrative heirarchy, procedure of membership, source of income, daily routine of Mahanth and general ascetics, branches, religious and public works etc. Spiritual heirarchy of some of the organisations under study have been given in detail along with organisations. All the ascetics of Ramanand Sampradaya, literate or illiterate can tell the spiritual heirarchy of his organisation. Some of the Organisations have formed a Trust for smooth functioning registered with Government of India. The religious festivals and Parikramas observed by the ascetics of almost all organisations is explained at one place at the end of this Chapter.

Chhoti-Chhawani-Baba Maniram Das Ki Chhawani

1. Chhoti-Chhawani or Baba Mani Ram Dasji Ki Chhawani

Spiritual heirarchy:

Ramanand
|
Anantanand
|
Payohari Srikrishnadas
|
Agradas
|
Ram Bhagwan Das
|
Lakshman Das
|
Mastram Das
|
Lakshmiram Das
|
Nandlal Das
|
Charan Das (Yodharam)
|
Hari Das
|
Vindukacharya Ram Prasad
|
Hanuman Nad
|
Maniram Das (Founder of Chhoti Chhawani)
|
Vaishnava Das
|
Ram Charan Das
|
Ram Sobha Das
|
Ram Manohar Das
|
Nritya Gopal Das (Present Mahanth)

History

Baba Mani Ram Dasjee established his Chhawani about 200 years ago. He was the disciple of Swami Hanuman Dasjee, who was one of the disciples of Swami Ram Prasadacharyajee, founder of Vendi Tilak and began the service of Sadhus. Hari Ram Dasjee joined Badasthan and engaged himself in the service of Sadhus. He used to take meal after feeding the Sadhus. One day he left the Sthan and went to Chitrakut, where Hanuman gave him order to resume Santseva on the bank of Saryu river. He returned to Ayodhya with an inner desire to serve the Saints He wanted to establish a Chhawani of the same. One day a gentleman was going by the side of a bullock cart putting on the image of Lord Hanuman, the axle of cart broke and the image fell on the ground. Even after great attempts the gentleman could not succeed to take the image out. Then Mani Ram Dasjee took it out, and established the image in the present Chhawani. Since then recitation of Valmiki Ramayan became a compulsory feature which is still continuing. The Chhawani gradually improved with the blessings of Hanumanjee. He served as Mahanth of this Maurusi Mutt upto 22 years and passed away in the year 1835 A.D.

Swami Vaishnava Dasjee become the Mahanth in the year 1836 A.D. who served upto 60 years as Mahanth. He was a Sidha saint. It is the belief of people that he was blessed with Gutka Sidhi by the help of which he travelled any distance within a short time. He left the world in 1896 A.D. Swami Ramcharan Dasjee was honoured as Mahanth of the Mutt in 1896 A.D. He was of the opinion that every Sadhu (ascetic) must know the religious performances of Virakta Vaishnavas. They should also empower themselves with the Sampradaya's Rules and Regulations. In his opinion service to saints is the greatest work of the world. The Mahanths are the servants of Saints, not the Lords. He died in the year 1906 A.D. Swami Ram Sobha Dasjee agreed to sit on the Gaddi on the request of all Sadhus of Ayodhya at the age of only 30 years. He expanded and renovated the Mutt. He took salvation in the year 1957 A.D. Ram Manohar Dasjee was honoured as the Vth Mahanth of the Mutt in the year 1957 A.D. After six years of his valuable services he left the world in the year 1963 A.D.

At present the great responsibility lies on the shoulder of a young Sadhu Swami Nritya Gopal Dasjee who sat on the Gaddi in the year 1963 A.D. Under his Mahanthship the Mutt is earning name and fame by leaps and bound. The spiritual heirarchy of the Mutt is as follows after the founder and detailed heirarchy is given at the beginning:

Mani Ram Dasjee	:	1813 A.D. to 1835 A.D.
↓		
Vaishnava Dasjee	:	1836 A.D. to 1896 A.D.
↓		
Ram Charan Dasjee	:	1896 A.D. to 1906 A.D.
↓		
Ram Sobha Dasjee	:	1906 A.D. to 1957 A.D.
↓		
Ram Manohar Dasjee	:	1957 A.D. to 1963 A.D.
↓		
Nritya Gopal Dasjee	:	1963 A.D. continuing

Present Position

The Organisation at present has a very big building with many rooms and two big halls. The halls accommodate nearly 300 ascetics of whom some reside in the specially constructed Mandapas with tin roof. There are several almirahs in the halls and in the Mandapas where the Sadhus and Vanprasthis keep their belongings. Only Vaishnavas are alloted with the almirah and rooms. A Vaishnava Vanprasthi offering Rs. 1000 (Rupees one thousand) or more is provided with the almirah. The amount once realised is enough to provide him boarding and lodging for his whole life.

There are special rooms for Mahanth, Adhikari, Kothari

and Pujari. There are also provisions for allotment of rooms to the visiting Sadhus. It is done by Mahanth himself. The building is being maintained annually. Four hundred and fifty ascetics and Vanprashthis are regularly residing in the Organisation. The Virakta Sadhus living unitedly there free from caste or linguistic prejudices belongs to different linguistic states like, Orissa, Bengal, Bihar, Gujarat, Maharastra, Punjab, Haryana, Jammu and Kashmir. The Maximum number of Sadhus are from Bihar and Madhya Pradesh.

Administrative Organisation

The Mathadhish known as Mahanth is the Supreme Head of the Chhawani and the official heirarchy runs down as follows: Next to Mahanth is Adhikari. The Chart given below clearly explains the official heirarchy of the Chhawani:

Chart Showing Administrative Heirarchy

Mahanth
(Swami Nritya Gopal Dasjee)
|
Adhikari (2)
(Anandram Dasjee)
(Vishwambhar Dasjee)
|
Kothari
(Baldeo Dasjee)
|
Pujari (5)
(Ram Rajya Das)
(Bajrang Das)
(Uddhawa Das)
(Govind Das)
(Prabhu Das)
|
Vyas (3)
(Swami Hari Acharya)
(Ram Prasad Shastri)

(Raghunath Das)
|
Kotwal
(Ram Kripal Das)
|
(Bagicha Adhikari
(Ram Deo Das)
|
Prasadia (2)
|
Jal Bharia (3)
|
Bhandari (25)
|
Gopala (4)

Adhikari	Next to Mahanth are two Adhikaris who administer the functioning of organisation on behalf of Mahanth.
Kothari	One Kothari, may be understood as a Storekeeper seeing his main job to look after the stores.
Pujari	There are five Pujaries, who are specialised in Shastric worship of the temple deity situated inside the Mutt. They are the experts in rites and rituals of the Sampradaya having a good knowledge of Sanskrit.
Vyas	There are three (3) Vyas, specialists of three different—Ramayans namely Valmiki Ramayan, Tulsi Ramayan and Bhaktmal Ramayan. They recite the Ramayan and holds Pravachan before the deity. They have their special seat known as Vyasasan.
Kotwal	One Kotwal having a great responsibility to

	check the unauthorised entry of Sadhus by asking Taksar and to look after Panghat the feeding arrangements.
Prasadia and Jalbharia	They are engaged in manual work.
Bhandari	There are 25 (twenty five) Bhandaries who are the cooks.

In addition to these there are ascetics living in the Chhawani.

Membership

A particular process is adopted for granting membership to new entrants—whenever a new person wants entry into the Chhawani, he approaches the Mahanth directly or through the ascetic of Sampradaya. He expresses the desire for initiation. The Mahanth allows him after watching for some time and getting confidential report about the new comer by the ascetics. If Mahanth is satisfied then he initiates the person following Pancha Samskara system and permanent membership is being allowed to him. The membership of Chhawani is open to all Ramanandi ascetics of Vaishnava Sampradaya. The person engaged in any immoral act or doing against the code of conducts of Organisation is immediately expelled by the Mahanth.

Sources of Income

Akasvrity is the main source of income. As the rain-falls from the sky, like the same whatsoever cash and kind comes to the Mutt abruptly from any unknown source is called Akasvrity.

Chharhwa—Disciples from different places offers Chharhwas to Guru—the Mahanth. These Chharhwas are of two types—

(1) *Monthly*

Offering ever not fixed but nearly Rs. 10 to Rs. 100 are sent by some disciples.

(2) *Occasional*

Some of the disciples visiting their Guru offers big amount above Rs. 1000 as Guru Dakshina when they meet the Mahanth.

The Chhawani has a broad range of followers nearly, 5,00,000 (Five lakhs) so offerings are received from them sooner or later. The Mahanth and other ascetics also earn wealth for Chhawani by delivering religious discourses on Ramayan at various places. The immovable properties like house, land etc. are now-a-days not being accepted by Mahanth even if any disciple willing to do so. The reason behind, as told by the Mahanth, is that the Organisation is of the view that the Sadhus are not required to take risk of these properties because there is every danger of being polluted. Such properties are sure to bring fights, litigations and quarrable confusions which are always to be avoided in a place of worship. Sitting for days, I have personally watched that money orders ranging from Rs. 10 to Rs. 100 (Rupees one hundred) have been received by the Mutt people on the average of Fifty (50) daily.

Daily Routine

Mahanth

Mahanth, Sri Nritya Gopal Dasjee, wakes up early in the morning at 4.00 A.M. and after bath sits in self-meditation for two hours i.e. upto 8.00 A.M. Then he goes to the temple for worship of the deity. Sri Ram and Hanuman, after finishing his puja he sits on his Gaddi where he meets the visitors, ascetics and general public. He discusses normally daily management work with the Mutt people. He takes his lunch at 12.00 noon and rests upto 2.00 p.m. Again he comes to his Gaddi, which is a special place covered with dear's skin and looks after Management work. He takes part in two Araties, one in morning and other in the evening. Then he participates in religious discourses organised at different places in between 7.00 p.m. to 8.00 p.m. where he delivers lectures on Ramayan.

Then he also visits other temples and finally go for sleep at 10.00 p.m.

Daily Routine

General Ascetics

As indicated, early, there are nearly 450 (four hundred and fifty) ascetics in the Chhawani. They get up early in the morning latest by 4.00 a.m. First of all they pray their deity Ram and Hanuman and then after finishing nature's call they take their bath either in the holy river Saryu or in the Chhawani, then engage themselves in worship and self-meditation for about three hours. Then they assemble in the temple for Arati, then they go for Amania where they clean rice, pulse etc. and keep vegetables ready for being cooked. This continues upto mid-day. Then after on the call for Panghat by Kotwal they sit in two or three rows. This call is known as Phanghat Sita Ram meaning thereby that all the Sadhus of Chhawani are invited for lunch. After lunch they sit for their own work, i.e. some of them counts beads, some go for little rest and some engage themselves in Kirtan. Again they gather in the temple in the evening at 7.00 p.m. and then they go to the different Mutts and temple for hearing religious discourses by different experts. Then they come back and go for sleep.

Branches of Mutta

This Chhawani is presently having 31 (thirty-one) branches at different parts of India in the 7 (Seven) States and 7 (Seven) branches at Ayodhya. These branches have only association with Chhawani of Guru-Shishya-Relation, otherwise they are totally free for management and development of their own. The list of the branches are given below:

Extent of Shishya (disciples)

The Chhawani is maintaining a very broad range of Shishyas belonging to India, Nepal, Fiji, Canada and Holland. The total number of Grihastha Shishya are approximately 5,00,000 (Five lakhs) and Virakta Shishya approximately 1000 (one thousand).

Branches at Ayodhya

Sl. No.	*Name of Mutt*	*Place*
1	2	3
1.	Ram Ratan Daskasthan	Basudeoghat
2.	Sarvabhaamjee Ka Sthan	Jankighat
3.	Ganga Bhawan	Jankighat
4.	Ramjeevan Daskasthan	Basudeoghat
5.	Ramayani Raghunath Daskasthan	Vibhisthan Kund
6.	Murli Dasjee Ka Sthan	Nayaghat
7.	Lakshman Ghat	Lakshman Ghat

Branches in India

Sl. No.	*Place of Mutt*	*Nos.*	*State*
1	2	3	4
1.	Varanasi	1	Uttar Pradesh
2.	Kanpur	1	"
3.	Jalon	2	"
4.	Jhansi	2	"
5.	Ayodhya	7	"
6.	Arrah	3	Bihar
7.	Balia	2	U.P.
8.	Places not known	5	Madhya Pradesh
9.	Hyderabad	1	Andhra Pradesh
10.	Places not known	2	Gujarat
11.	Places not known	3	Punjab
12.	Places not known	3	Jammu and Kashmir
13.	Ajamgarh	2	Uttar Pradesh
14.	Barabanki	2	"
15.	Lucknow	1	"
16.	Unnaon	1	"

The Chhawani's Shishya are developing by leaps and bound. In the year 1973 when I conducted the first research work that time the total number of Shishya was 40,000 (Forty thousand only) within the span of six years when I conducted the present study in the year 1979 the number increased to Five (5) Lakhs. This gives an idea that the Mahanth and ascetics have earned a good name and people are coming into Vaishnavite fold.

Religious and Public Works

The Chhawani plays an important role in the religious preachings for the development of Hinduism in general and Vaishnavism in particular. Sadhus well versed in religious commentaries move from place to place and organises Ramarchas, Kirtans, explains the importance of Vaishnavism among their disciples and other interested persons. The Mahanth takes special interest in the religious work. He organises Katha-Varta, Ramdhun, Astayam, Bharat-Yatras, Ramarchas. Special arrangements are being made at the time of Bharat Yatras which is a march of Sadhus from Ayodhya to Chitrakut. In this nearly thousands of ascetics moves reciting Ram Nam etc. He also organises Navah i.e. recital of Ramayan for nine days. There are a number of note-worthy works of the Chhawani for the benefit of general public as given below:

1. Two medical centres, one of Ayurvedic medicines and one of Homeopathic medicines are running where the medicines are being provided free of cost to the patients. As per my observations at both the centres 100 (one hundred) patients are treated daily.
2. One Sanskrit School for the teaching of Grammar, Astrology, Vedanta and Veda is running with 40 (Forty) students sponsored by the Chhawani.
3. Valmiki Research Centre and Library:

   This is a praise-worthy work of the Chhawani. One Valmiki Bhawan has been constructed with at the cost of nearly Rs. 80 Lakhs (Rupees Eighty lakhs) just opposites the Chhawani with the Slokas of Valmiki Ramayan inscribed on marble and fitted on the walls of it. Here, one library with 20,000 (Twenty thousand) books on religion and special Valmiki Research Centre in a religio-cultural monuments of the country. This is a praise-worthy contribution for public and considered as a remarkable cultural offer of Chhawani to the people.

2. Lakshman Kila

Spiritual Heirarchy

Ramanand	Shanker Das
|	|
Sursuranand	Jiva Ram (Yugal Priya)
|	|
Madhawanand	Yugalananya Sharan (Founder of Lakshman Kila)
|	|
Garibanand	Ramodar Sharan
|	|
Lakshmi Das	Ram Baijnath Sharan
|	|
Gopal Das	Lakhanlal Sharan
|	|
Narhari Das	Ramdeo Sharan
|	|
Kewal Kuba Ram	Sita Ram Sharan (Present)
|	
Damodar Das	
|	
Hriday Ram	
|	
Kripa Ram	
|	
Ratnakar	
|	
Nripati Das	

History

Lakshman Kila is a very famous ascetic organisation of Ramanandi Sampradaya which is being graced by the ascetics of highest order for the last two centuries. This monastry was founded by a great Saint, Swami Yuglananya Sharanjee Maharaj. Swamijee was born in a Saraswat Brahmin family on Kartik Sukla Saptami 1875 V.S. at Islampur in Patna District of Bihar. From the very childhood he showed signs of saintly activities and his personality was robust. He was a great musician having an inner desire for a life of purity and perfection, service and devotion. He was disciple of Sri Yugalprayajee Maharaj and so he become Yuglananya Sharanjee. He used to live in supreme bliss Brahmanand, and no worldly affairs could attract him ever.

Arriving at Ayodhya he enjoyed perfect pleasure and then he moved there from lane to lane singing and dancing with the pious names of Sri Ram Janki, his brother and Hanuman. After sometime he practised Maunavrata (silence) on the bank of Saryu river for fourteen months, enchanting only Sita Ram. In course of time he constructed a Ram Janki temple. Being deeply impressed by the spiritual achievements of this pious soul, Queen Victoria gave him this Kila (Fortess) formerly known as Kila Mubarak without any taxation on it. From that very time this Kila which stands on the Lakshman Ghat of Saryu river becomes famous as Lakshman Kila.

In 1922 V.S. Maharaja of Rivan built the present temple inside the organisation.

Present Organisation

Lakshman Kila has its own organisation headed by the Kiladhish who is the Chief of the Mutt. There are two Deputy Chiefs known as Adhikari. Among ten administrative bodies of the Mutt there are four Bhandaries besides, Vyavasthapak and Kothari, Bhandaries are assisted by four others. The religious officials are pujaries numbering five in all. The

Kathavyas is engaged for religious discourses on Ramayan. Munim looks after the accounts. In addition, there are three drivers and thirty (30) other members. Previously the Head Office was in Chirain village of Chhapra District in Bihar, but now-a-days it has been shifted to Kila. A printing press of its own has a special attraction as it shows the Kila's interest in expressing news and views and guiding the Vaishnavites through the magazines Awadh Sandesh.

This Mutt is a Maurusi Mutt run under two trusts named Ram Janki Mandir Trust and Lakshman Kila Trust.

At present 50 (Fifty) ascetics are permanent residents in the Mutt. On special occasions number vary from 100 and above.

Branches of the Mutt

The Mutt has 26 (twenty-six) branches at various places like Ayodhya, Janakpur, Sitamarhi and Fiji. The list is given below:

Chart Showing the Branches of Lakshman Kila

	Sl. No.	*Name of the Mutt*	*Location*
At Ayodhya	1.	Sadguru Sadan	Gola Ghat
	2.	Hanumat Niwas	Gola Bazar
	3.	Rin Mochan Ghat	Rin Mochan Ghat
	4.	Mithila Kunj	Gola Bazar
	5.	Videhja Dulhani Kunj	"
	6.	Siyavar Kunj	"
	7.	Saryu Kunj	"
	8.	Purusṣottam Bhawan	"
	9.	Sadguru Niwas	Vibhishan Kund
	10.	Sadguru Kuti	"
	11.	Ram Dham	Gola Bazar
	12.	Shyam Dham	"
	13.	Hanumat Sadan	"
	14.	Siva Ram Kila	Jhumki Ghat

	15.	Jankivar Bhawan	Gola Ghat
	16.	Hanumat Sadan	Swargdwar
At Ajankur in	17.	Peelee Kuti	Sita Marhi
Nepal	18.	Raghwandra Shansathan	"
	19.	Sidh Babasthan	"
	20.	Chhoti Kutia	"
In Fiji	21.	Siya Kunj	Fiji

Sources of Income

The Lakshman Kila is financial well-established as it commands 500 (Five hundred) acres of land in Uttar Pradesh, 300 (Three hundred) acres were donated by Raja of Gonda in Basti District and 300 (Three hundred) acres are at Barahia in Bihar. The land at Barahia has been sold now. It has a big garden also at Makdumpur in Faizabad, Uttar Pradesh. Time to time notable and ordinary donations are also received by the Mahanth. Awadh Sandesh also gives good sale. A sample chart of income and expenditure for a year is given below. At present there are three vehicles, two jeeps and one car in the organisation.

Daily Routine

Mahanth

Sixty (60) years old Mahanth popularly known as Kiladhish Sri Sita Ram Sharanjee walks early in the morning for about six (6) miles after rising at the Brahma Muhurt. On return, he takes his bath and worships Lord. He counts the bead i.e. Jap of Sita Ram one lakh daily. His mid-day is spent in Swadhyaya and Sanskrit teaching. In the evening he delivers religious discourses on Ramayan and then visits Kanak Bhawan daily.

Daily Routine

General Ascetics

Daily routine of ascetics are the same as that of the ascetics of Mani Ram Das Kichhavani.

Followers of the Mutt

The Organisation patronises approximately 10,000 (Ten Thousand) followers from the States of Bihar, Uttar Pradesh, Rajasthan, Nepal, Fiji etc. The number of followers from Bihar is the highest. Kiladhish opines that the Ramanand Sampradaya is flourishing due to the devotees from Bihar. The Major number comes from the districts like Muzzafarpur, Darbhanga Monghyr, Sita Marhi, Gaya, Patna, Hazaribagh, Begusarai and Nalanda. As per information given by Kiladhish the followers belongs to the following castes:

Bhumihar, Khitriya, Kayastha, from Uttar Pradesh, Bihar, Marwaries from West Bengal (Calcutta and Bihar), Agarwal from Uttar Pradesh and Rajasthan.

Activities of Organisation and People

The ascetics of Kila takes interest in religious and social activities and shows active association with the Hindu religion. They work for the development of Hindu (Vedic) ideas and never remain silent wherever and whenever attack in any shape on Hinduism is learnt by the members of the Mutt or Kiladhish himself. Kiladhish is also not completely disinterested with the political activities of the day because for the defence of his ideas and ideals it is but necessary, perhaps he feels to have an eye open towards the present day activities of the world. But so far as it could be guessed and gathered during the research the Kiladhish and the ascetics are not actively associated with politics. The Kiladhish takes keen interest in the treatment of poor patients and donates good amount of money to different hospitals at Ayodhya. The organisation also grants scholarships to the poor and meritorious students and also arranges food for them. Among Mahanths of Ayodhya he commands good respect.

3. Badi-Chhawani-Baba Raghunath Dasjee Ki Chhawani

Spiritual Heirarchy:

Ramanand
|
Bhawanand
|
Anubhavanand
|
Virajnand
|
Balanand (Founder of Laskari Tilak)
|
Vithalanand
|
Ballabhanand
|
Brahmanand
|
Mandas
|
Mansaram Das
|
Ram Raghunath Das
|
Ram Chandra Das
|
Mani Baldeo Das
|
Raghunath Das (Founder of Baddi Chhawani)
|
Jaggannath Das
|
Iswar Das
|
Kaushal Kishore Das
|
Ram Pratap Das (Present)

History

Baba Raghunath Dasjee was the founder of this Mutt. He was formerly a Sepoy in the British Army. He became the disciple of Maharaj Baldeo Dasjee. When he was in the Army an incident occurred. While going on his duty he once entered into a temple where Harikirtan was going on. He also took part in the same and practically forgot his duty. At the end of Kirtan he found himself late and rushed to the Sergent begging excuse for the mistake. But there, to his utter surprise, he heard the Sergent, that he was marked present and was found on duty and his successor had already taken the charge from him. The incident moved him so much that he submitted his resignation and came to Ayodhya with the feeling that Lord Rama performed his duty and took the pain. He started meditation at Sheetal Amarai from where he came to the present place and become famous as a Sidhapurush.

Once a lady approached him and requested to arrange a Bhandara with a Adhela. He agreed and used her Adhela to purchase Haldi and in this way Bhandara was performed. Next time the same lady came and offered Rupees Six thousand. The amount was used in the construction of the Mutt which was established in the year 1840 A.D. After him the spiritual heirarchy of Mahanth is as follows:

Baba Raghunath Dasjee
|
Swami Jaggannath Dasjee
|
Iswar Dasjee
|
Kaushal Kishore Dasjee
|
Ram Pratap Dasjee (Present)

Present Organisation

The Mutt has a huge campus with 100 rooms, 14 temples and a Library building. This is a Maurusi Mutt. The Mahanth, Adhikari and the following ascetics are in-charge of the administration.

Sl. No.	*Designation*	*Nos.*
1.	Pujari	14
2.	Mukhtar	5
3.	Kothari	3
4.	Bhandari	20
5.	Parkhatia	14

About 300 (three hundred) ascetics are getting food daily. Most of the ascetics do not take keen interest in worship but are engaged in manual works like wood-cutting, cooking, looking after cows etc. The ascetics wear Laskari Tilak on their forehead. Mahanth and other officials were approached several times but they never gave any information and said that our organisation works on Akashvriti as we have nothing to inform you, seeing the organisational appointments a man can easily guess the prosperity of the Mutt. At the time of Bhandaras this Mutt surpasses the expenditure of all the Muttas at Ayodhya.

This Mutt is staunch supporter of caste system and so they observe strictness in the appointment of executives. They appoint only Brahmin caste ascetics as Pujari and cook and only ascetics belonging to touchable castes are appointed as executives. The sense of untouchability from the lower castes has been observed being strictly maintained by the Mutt people.

Branches of the Mutt

The Mutt has 150 (one hundred and fifty) branches at various places in India. At Ayodhya it has 8 (eight) branches as follows:

Chart of Branches of Mutt

Sl. No.	*Name*	*Place*
1	2	3
1.	Maunijee Ki Chhawani	Ramghat
2.	Sanatan Mandir	"
3.	Mai Bada	"
4.	Mani Parvat	Mani Parvat
5.	Pandey Jee Ka Mandir	Pramodvan
6.	Gaya Mandir	"
7.	Bhakt Mal Mandir	Raiganj
8.	Rajendra Bhawan	Kannuganj

Sources of Income

It was told that the only source is Akashvriti. Although exact information could not be gathered from the Mutt, I came to know from the neighbours that the Mutt has 20 (twenty) bighas of land at Gonda, and 100 (one hundred) bighas of land an Manjha of Uttar Pradesh. As I observed by sitting at Mutt and interviewing the Postman I came to know that nearly 100 (one hundred) money orders are pouring down daily varying from the range of Rs. 5 to Rs. 500 from its followers who are approximately 80,000 (Eighty thousand) in numbers. The majority comes from Bihar, Madhya Pradesh, Rajasthan and other parts of India.

Mutt Followers

At present there are 80,000 (Eighty thousand) followers of the Mutt. In the year 1973 the number was only 50,000 (Fifty thousand). It shows the development of Organisation and increase of followers 30,000 (Thirty thousand) within the span of Six (6) years. The majority comes from the State of Bihar, Madhya Pradesh and Rajasthan.

Daily Routine

Early in the morning the working in Mutt starts and the

ascetics of the Mutt gather at one place in the Mutt temple for Arati at 7.30 a.m. After that they engage themselves in Bhajan-Puja for an hour. Again at 9.00 a.m. they gather in the temple for Arati from where they go for Amania work. Amania is cleaning the materials for food and Puja. Then they are allowed to the work of their own. At 2.00 p.m. they assemble at the Mutt for Panghat and after taking their lunch they become free again. In this time, they move from one place to another to meet other ascetics of other Organisations. At 7.00 p.m. again they attend Arati in the Mutt and go for their own Japa, Swadhyaya or attend Katha Pravachan at different places and then they take rest.

4. Bada-Sthan-Ram Prasadacharya Ka Sthan

Spiritual Heirarchy:

Ramanand
|
Anantanand
|
Payohari Krishna Das
|
Agradas
|
Ram Bhagwan Das
|
Lakshman Das
|
Mastaram
|
Lakshmiram Das
|
Nandlal Das
|
Charan Das (Yodharam)
|
Hari Das
|

Vindukacharya Ram Prasad (Founder of Badasthan)
|
Raghunath Frasad
|
Janki Prasad
|
Ayodhya Prasad
|
Hariudhana Prasad
|
Sarju Prasad
|
Raghava Prasad
|
Gopal Prasad
|
Ram Mandhar
|
Raghubar Prasad
|
Ram Kripal Das (Present)

History

This organisation was established by Swami Ram Prasadjee, founder of Bendi Tilak in 1960 V.S. During the ninth Mahanth of heirarchy, Swami Ram Manohar Dasjee in 1937 A.D. extension work took place on a large scale. It is having a very big Kothar and a nice temple. This temple was renovated again by the Tenth Mahanth Swami Raghubir Prasadjee. This is one of the oldest ascetics Centre at Ayodhya.

Present Organisation

The Mutt has a very huge building in Ramkot area of Ayodhya with four temples inside it. It has a large number of its followers. The present organisation is as follows:

Mahanth
Ram Kripal Das
|
Pujari (4)
(Bishwambhar Das)
(Raghubir Das)
(Ramsevak Das)
(Damodar Das)
|
Kothari (1)
(Sri Sheo Ram Das)
|
Bhandari (4)
|
Parkatia (1)
|
Jalbharia (3)
|
Kotwal (1)
(Ram Bilash Das)

This Organisation is having huge property but the Mahanth or other ascetic never gave any figure about it. At present, only 30 (thirty) ascetics are residing in the Mutt. The daily routine of the Mutt people is same as of Chhoti Chhawani. One peculiarity is that one Pujari is offering 1000 (one thousand) Tulsi leaves to the deity every day.

Branches of Mutt

Sl. No.	*Name of Organisation*	*Location*
1	2	3
1.	Pauharijee Ka Sthan	Mani Parvat
2.	Jankighat (Badighat)	Janki Ghat
3.	Janki Niwas	Pramod Van
4.	Jal Parnale	Pramod Van

5.	Baghi Sthan	Vibheesan Kund
6.	Chhoti Chhawani	Basudeo Ghat
7.	Jharana Bagia	Mani Parvat

5. Ramballabha Sharan Kunj

Spiritual Heirarchy

Ramanand
|
Yoganand
|
Mayanand
|
Tulsi Das
Bhagwati
|
Nayan Ram
|
Kham Chawgani
|
Udhao Maidani
|
Khem Das
|
Ram Das
|
Lakshuman Das
|
Deva Das
|
Balkrishna Das
|
Beni Das
|
Shravan Das
|
Ram Bachan Das
|
Pt. Ramvallabha Sharan
|
Ram Padarath Das 'Vedanti'
|
Harnam Das Vedanti (Present)

History

This famous Ramanandi Mutt at Ayodhya was established by Sri Ram Ballabha Sharanjee in the year 1912 A.D. The name at the time of foundation was Madhukar Niwas. He organised a Trust named Janaki Jiwan Trust in the year 1939 A.D. with the following as Trustees:

1. Ram Padarath Dasjee Vedanti

Ram Ballabha Kunj, Ayodhya.

2. Mahanth Ram Sobha Dasjee
Chhoti Chhawani, Ayodhya.
3. Raja Bahadur Harihar Prasad Narayan Singh
Amawan, Tekari, Bihar.
4. Raja Bahadur Guru Mahadeo Sahab Shahi
Hathuwa, Chhapra, Bihar.
5. Pandit Ram Kishore Shukla, Advocate
Ayodhya.

Sri Ram Ballabha Sharanjee was also the President of Bharat Sadhu Samaj. After him the spiritual heirarchy of the Mutt is as follows:

Ram Ballabha Sharan
|
Ram Padarath Das 'Vedanti'
|
Harnam Dasjee Vedanti (Present)

This Organisation is popularly known as Vedantijee Ka Sthan.

Present Organisation

The present Mutt is having a large building complex. In the main building the image of Ram and Sita is placed, made up of white marble. The head is Mahanth Harnam Dasjee Vedanti, after him the heirarchy is as follows:

Mahanth
(Harnam Dasjee Vedanti)
|
Adhikari
(Sri Ghanshyam Dasjee)
|
Pujari (10)
|

Bhandari (12)
|
Kothari (2)
|
Parkatia (10)
|
Jalbharia (10)
|
Gosewak (15)
|
Bag Sevak (3)

About 30 (thirty) ascetics are residing and taking food in the Organisation daily. The organisation is Hakimi in nature where Mahanth is appointed by the Trustees. The name of Organisation at the time of foundation was Madhukar Niwas and now it has been changed to Ram Ballabh Sharan Kunj. It is run under a Trust name—*Janki Jiwan Trust* established in the year 1939 A.D. The entire property is now under Trust. The selection of Mahanth is being done by the Trustees. Mahanth must be a good man of Brahmin family without any claim against his character. If no Shishya of Sthan is capable, it is the power of Trustees to select one Mahanth from any other Organisation of Ramanandi Sampradaya. The Pujari also should be Brahmin who will perform Puja with Ramanandi method.

The present Trustees are:

1. Sri Harnam Dasjee Vedanti,
   Mahanth,
   Ram Ballabha Sharan Kunj,
   Ayodhya.
2. Sri Mahanth Nritya Gopal Dasjee,
   Mani Ram Das Ki Chhawani,
   Ayodhya.

3. Raja Raghuvansh Mani Prasad Narayan Singh, Amavan, Tekari, Bihar.
   and two others.

Hanuman Vatika and Hanuman Bag are two other huge buildings of this organisation. Service of Sadhu is the main motto of this organisation.

Sources of Income

Like other ascetic organisations, the Akasvriti is the source of income for this Organisation also, but this Mutt possess nearly 250 acres of land at different places as given below. While the Trust was formed in the year 1939 A.D. at that time the property under the Trust was as follows:

Property in Uttar Pradesh	:	Rs. 10,000
Property in Bihar	:	Rs. 21,000
Buildings	:	(a) Hanuman Vatika
		(b) Hanuman Bag

Land Under Cultivation

	Place	*Bigha*	*Biswa*	*Dhur*
1.	Miranpur, Awadh	3+3	4	10
2.	Dindayalpur, Bhagalpur	8	13	15
3.	Keshwa, Bhagalpur	2	10	11
4.	Keshwa, Bhagalpur	19	16	3
5.	Keshwa Bhagalpur	5	—	16
6.	Dalsingh Sarai	1	9	10
7.	Dalsingh Sarai	16	—	10
8.	Dalsingh Sarai	2	—	15
9.	Sahpur	1	12	—
10.	Gaya	1	98	—
11.	Tekari (Sansi)	52	4	6
12.	Tekari (Kutlupur)	72	15	14
	Total	248	1	15

Cash: Rs. 59,813.85 and other materials of Gold and Silver.

Social Work

Sanskrit College

To its credit this Organisation runs a Sanskrit College named Sadharum Vivardhini Sanskrit Mahavidyalaya affiliated to Dr. Sampuranand Sanskrit University, Kashi. In this college, the study is upto Acharya. There are 7 paid teachers and 50 (Fifty) students. The students are provided with free food and shelter by the Organisation.

Gosala

There is a huge Gosala with 40 (forty) cows at present. This organisation has popularised Ramarcha Puja in the Hindus of the country.

Library

There is a Library called Ram Ballabha Pustakalaya having huge collections of books on Vaishnava Dharma. To propagate the essence of Vaishnavism very recently they have organised one Sadgrantha-Prachar-Kendra in the Mutt with Sri Janki Dasjee Vaishnava as founder.

Branches of Mutta

This Organisation has Six (6) Branches at Ayodhya, Four (4) Branches at Madhya Pradesh, Two (2) in Rajasthan and Two (2) in Bihar State.

Branches at Ayodhya are:

1. Hanuman Vatika
2. Hanuman Bag
3. Sukla Mandir
4. Ichha Mandir
5. Chhatuh Sampradaya Sthan

6. Kaushilesh Sadan

History

There is an important Mutt of Ramanuja Sampradaya at

Katra which is known as Kaushilesh Sadan and also as Acharya Mutt. Tridandi Swami has established Lakshmi Narayan Temple at Charitravan in Buxar and this Mutt of Ayodhya is one of its branches. In the year 1963 A.D., the Kaushilesh Sadan was renovated by Jagatguru Swami Ram Narayancharyajee Vedant Martand is now 56 (fifty-six) years old. Kaushilesh Sadan is not only a Mutt, but it is a temple also. The peculiarity of this Sadan exists in the difficulty of differentiation between the Mutt and temple as both are each others compliments. It may be said that this Sadan is a good example of power equivalence. Here the Mathadhish or Mahanth is the temple head also.

Organisation

A Trust known as Dharmadaya Trust governs this Mutt. The Trust's President is Antarah Jagadguru Swami Ram Narayanacharyajee. There are other 14 (Fourteen) Executives Members of the Trust. All these members are from the different parts of the country, who attend the meetings whenever the President calls it. The meeting is held not only at Ayodhya but also outside the place for the meeting is selected as desired by the Executives. The head of the Mutt is known as Mahanth who enjoys Supreme power i.e. to say is all-in-all of the Mutt.

Mantri

Mantri is the next authority, who is selected by the Trustees. It is remarkable point that while the Mahanth can be nominated by the previous Mahanth, the Mantri can only be appointed by the Trustees and not only on the sweet will of the Mahanth.

There are Two (2) Pujaris of whom one is the Pradhan and another an Assistant. The Pradhan Pujari only has got the right to open the temple and responsibility for all the performances of the Mutt temple lies with him. Interference in his work by any one is strictly prohibited. It is essential for a Pujari to be a Saryupari Brahmin having at least Shastri degree in Sanskrit and possessing ample knowledge of Karma Kanda. Of course there is no age limit for him. Neither is he required to be alife-long celibate. He may marry whenever, but not wherever he likes.

For Kotharies, there are two (2) Posts and they look after Kothar i.e. the Store where the cooking materials are stored. There are three Rasoiyas whose duty is to cook Prasad with all purity as established by the Sampradaya. Any slip in performance of duty is taken to bring impurity in Prasad and is not accepted. As such the cooks remain ever vigilant.

It is for the Mantri to select Pujaries, Kotharis and Rasoiyas. For the membership only those touchables choose the Mahanth who offer Dakchhina to him. The another source of income is Chharhwa specially during the time of his religious discourses on Ramayan, Gita, Bhagwat etc. Sometimes this kind of Chharhwa amounts upto three to four lakhs also. Once in a Pandal arranged by Jaipur Naresh the Mahanth got three lakhs of rupees as Chharhwa but he accepted only 10,000 (Ten thousand) and donated the rest to the local temple.

Daily Routine

This Mutt or the Mandir is opened regularly by the Pujari at 4.30 p.m. in the morning and Mangal Arati takes place at 5.00 a.m. Again at 8.00 a.m. Shrinagar Arati is performed after the performance of the Puja.

The Pujari offer Bhog at 11.00 a.m. and closes the door. The Mutt re-opens at 4.00 p.m. and it is known as Utthapan. The Arati takes places at 9.00 a.m. again and the Mandir closes at 10.00 p.m. All the people of the Mutt gather in the main temple at the time of Arati and from there they go to Amania except the Mahanth, Mantri and the Pujari. All the Mandir performances are performed by the Pujari and his helpers. While the Mantri looks after financial and administrative business the all-in-all of the Mutt is Mahanth, but the remains practically outside Ayodhya keeping himself busy in Katha, Pravachan etc. at different places.

7. Vijay Raghaw

There is a Mutt at Srinagar Hat known as Vijay Raghaw. The building is not so well-maintained although it is quite good looking from outside. Even now there is no provision for electricity there and the reason behind it, as put-forth by the Mahanth is quite amusing. The belief there is that the Tejah Prakash or the bright light of Lord Vishnu showed never be dis-illusioned by these worldly lights. The Mutt itself is a temple which was established Eighty (80) years before by Sri Bal Ram Swami, the Guru of the present Mahanth. The Mahanth is the follower of Acharya Sampradaya and is himself disciple of Rangji, the Mahanth of Brindavan. The statues of the deity in the temple are very old and were brought by Pandit Sri Bhagwatacharya Shastri from the outside of Puruvali in Pachh Parimal Koel Area of Madras.

Organisation

The incharge of the Mutt is the Mahanth himself and there are two Pujaries who are required to perform all the religious performances of the temple. The Mahanth and the Pujaries are Brahmin by Caste. The Two (2) Bhandaries who are also Brahmin by Caste are required to cook the food of the Mutt people. The real Administrative Officer of the Mutt is Adhikari, whose duty is to look after the administration of the Mutt and its branches at Brindavan. The other members of the Mutt numbering about 25 (Twenty-five) of whom some are ascetics and some are the students of different Pathasalas. The students are provided with free food, clothing and other needfuls and after having finished the study they become ascetics in the very Mutt. The founder of the Mutt Sri Bal Ram Swami had established a Trust named as Sri Bal Ram Dharmetu Trust having five (5) members in it.

The members were at first selected by the Swamiji, but

now-a-days whenever any casual vacancy occurs the members themselves co-opt a new Trustee.

Among the present members there are:

A Marwari Brahmin from Calcutta, One from Gorakhpur, the Mahanth of the Brindavan temple, and the fourth from Bombay, besides the present Mahanth of the Mutt. All the members are Brahmin by Caste and have no important role in the Mutt's administration. The Trustees meet annually in Chaitra or in Sharavan before whom the annual account is placed by the Ṁahanth.

Festival, Daily Routine

Among the important festivals, Narsingha Chatturdasi and Vaman Dwadasi are important, Vaman Dwadashi is celebrated in the month of Bhadrapada on the twelfth day (12th) of Suklapaksha in the memory of Vamanavatara of Vishnu. The daily routine of Mutt people is parallel to that of the members of Kaushilesh Sadan and no remarkable difference was observed.

Important Festivals Observed by Vaishnava Ascetics at Ayodhya

Most of the Hindu festivals are celebrated by ascetics at Ayodhya specially related to Ram, Sita and Vishnu. Some festivals like Ramnawami and Vivah Panchami are observed with great pomp and show and attract the largest number of pilgrims from every nook and corners of India and Nepal. These festivals are described below:

Kumbha

The greatest festival of ascetics is Kumbha. The detailed study have been done by Surjeet Sinha and B.N. Saraswati (Sinha, 1978). Therefore, I have omitted the same.

Ram Nawami

This festival is performed on ninth day of the light-fortnight of Chaitra (April). The festival starts from first day i.e. Pratipada and continues upto ninth day (Nawami) of the said fortnight. All Mutt-Temples are cleaned, white-washed and decorated during the period. The ascetics becomes very busy and they spend most of their time in Bhajan-Kirtan and in arranging different religious functions during the period for pilgrims. The temples remain open from early in the morning from 4.00 a.m. upto late in the night. The ascetics of Organisations arrange Ramlila, Bhajan, Nawah Parayan of Ramcharit Manas and Balmiki Ramayan. In the evening religious discourses are organised where they deliver lectures on different aspects of Ram-Charita. Millions of pilgrims gather at Ayodhya and take holy-bath at Saryu river and visit all Mutt and temples to a pay reverence.

Vivah Panchami

This is the second biggest festival falls on the Fifth (5th) day of light fortnight in the month of Agrahan (November-December). The ascetics celebrate the marriage anniversary of Ram-Sita. Organisation in Lakshman Kila invites all the Organisations. This is organised on a very large scale. For the last two (2) years Mahanth Sita Ram Sharanjee is organising Barat which starts from Ayodhya along with ascetics and devotees and reaches Janakpur in Nepal, the father's place of Sita. The image of Ram is taken in procession as Bridegroom. This is largely participated by the ascetics of Rasiko-Paasana. The Pilgrim. Kirtaniyas sing songs and play drums before the departure of Barat.

At Badasthan, ascetics invite Ramlila party. Every day after Sandhya Arati, Ramlila is performed, attended by thousands of pilgrims. It is performed from 7.00 p.m. to 10.00 p.m. The next day of marriage, they take out Janki which is held in Sabha Mandap of the Mutt. The image of Ram and Sita is placed in a Jhula. Ascetics, Mahanth surrounds the Jhula. Much money is spent for the purpose. At first, the Mahanth of Badasthan swings the Jhula, then it is repeated by the ascetics and devotees. Just near the Jhula a Kathavachak recites Ram Charit Manas. This continues upto 12.00 Clock in the midnight. The bridegroom (Ram) and bride (Sita) retire of the night.

Guru Purnima

This is celebrated in each and every ascetic Organisations at Ayodhya. It falls on the full-moon day in the month of Ashad (June-July). The ascetics and their followers gather at their Gurusthan to pay reverence to their respective Guru. They keep fast on the day from morning till the worship of Guru. The process of worship is same as the deity as per belief, Guru Dev Bhava i.e. Guru is the God like. At first the ascetics take bath in Saryu river and finish their normal Dhyan and Jap then come to Guru. The Guru uses to wear new clothes and sits on well decorated Gaddi facing North or East direction. The disciples of first perform Arati with camphor and then offer flowers on the forehead mark (Tilak) of the Guru. Then they offer Bhog (sweets, fruits etc.), new cloths and money as Guru Dakshina. Then they wash feet of Guru in a pot with water. This water is called Charanamrit, which they spray on their body starting from forehead and the remaining water is drunk by them. It is their staunch belief that by drinking this water they will earn Gurukripa i.e. teacher's blessings, as well as Punya. At last they perform Sastang-Dandawat at Guru's feet. The Guru offers Bhandara in his organisation for all their disciples, irrespective of caste, sex and creed. On this occasion one can see the Vaishnava ascetics moving in all corners of Ayodhya. It can be said that Guru Purnima is the most sacred day for ascetics.

Annakut

This festival falls on the first day of light fortnight in the month of Kartik (October-November) i.e. next day of Deepavali. This is celebrated with great pomp in the Organisations of Ramanuj Sampradaya. On this day, Raj Bhog contains 108 (one hundred and eight) kinds of food materials, all vegetarian.

Bhandara is also organised for Mahanths and ascetics of all Organisations at Ayodhya.

Founder's Death Anniversaries

All Ramanandi ascetic Organisations at Ayodhya Organise Bhandara on the death anniversaries of the founder. These Bhandaras are participated by ascetics and guests. All present get the food and Dakshina. Mahanths of different Organisations sit in one Panghat and other ascetics in another. The cost of these types of Bhandara sometimes exceeds Rupees One Lakh even.

In addition to all the above festivals ascetics also observe the following festivals though in a simple manner:

Ramanuj Jayanti	:	Baisakh Sukla Panchami
Janki Nawami	:	Baisakh Sukla Nawami
Nrisingh Jayanti	:	Baisakh Sukla Chaturdashi
Janmastami	:	Bhadra Krishna Astami
Sharad Purnima	:	Ashwin Sukla Purnima
Hanuman Jayanti	:	Kartik Krishna Trayodashi
Ramanand Jayanti	:	Magh-Sukla Shashti.

Other festive occasions are Parikramas.

Parikrama means the circumbulation of deity or the religious place. Parikrama is the best method of blotting out all sins committed by individuals. The Parikramas are done in clock-wise directions. Four types of Parikramas are in practice at Ayodhya as described below:

(i) ***Brihad Parikrama***

This is also called Eighty-Four (84) Koshi Parikrama. It starts on full moon day of Chaitra from Manorama Tirth, God and terminates at the same place covering the places as resting centre on Janki Nawami as shown in the List-I. The total distance covered during this circumbulation is 168 (one hundred and sixty-eight) Miles.

1. *Brihad (168 Miles)*

1. Manorama Tirth
2. Ram Rekha
3. Shishya Sring
4. Gossain Ganj
5. Jahali Ashram
6. Surya Kund (Darab Ganj)
7. Nandigram
8. Astik Ashram
9. Janmajai Kund
10. Amani Ganj
11. Misir Ka Purba
12. Lakhanipur
13. Patranga
14. Kamiyar
15. Sukhar Khetra
16. Uttari Bhawani
17. Amdahi Ramghat
18. Gokul Dham
19. Kutila Sangam
20. Nawab Ganj
21. Nagwa
22. Sikandarpur
23. Manorama Tirth

(ii) ***Madhyam Parikrama***

This is called Fourteen (14) Koshi Parikrama. This starts on ninth (9th) day of bright fortnight in Kartik month i.e. Akshay Nawami from Swargdwar, Ayodhya. The devotees proceed Seven (7) Miles towards the bank of Saryu river and then touching the places given in List-II. This Parikrama is one day (24 hours) affairs. This attracts a large number of people. Some times number exceeds than Eight (8) Lakhs and the total distance covered during this circumbulation is 28 (twenty-eight) Miles. Places covered are as under:

Madhyam (28 Miles)

1. Niwajpur
2. Mukaram Nagar
3. Darshan Nagar
4. Kushmaha
5. Janaura
6. Khojanpur
7. Nirmal Kund
8. Guptar Ghat
9. Chakratirth
10. Brahma Kund
11. Kaushilya Ghat
12. Kaikai Ghat
13. Raj Ghat
14. Rinmochan Ghat
15. Pap Mochan Ghat
16. Swargdwar.

(iii) ***Laghu Parikrama***

This is called Panch Koshi Parikrama or Antergrihi. This has a route of Ten (10) Miles surrounding Ayodhya town. This is finished within 12 (twelve) hours. It starts from Swargdwar on second day after Madhyam Parikrama i.e. Eleventh (11th) day of Light Fortnight in Kartik month and covering places given in List-III under the same head terminates at Swargdwar. It is not essential to start from Swargdwar. A person can start from any place on the routs and will end it at the same place:

Laghu (10 Miles)

1. Swargdwar
2. Mauniji Ki Chhawani
3. Renopali
4. Janki Bag
5. Rinmochan Ghat
6. Pap Mochan Ghat
7. Lakshman Ghat
8. Swargdwar.

(iv) ***Ramkoti Parikrama***

It covers a routs of Five (5) Miles i.e. of entire Ramkot area of Ayodhya. It starts from Vashishta Kund and moving through Janki Ghat, Ram Ghat, Datun Kund and it terminates at the Vashishta Kund. It is a general routine of Vaishnava ascetics of Ayodhya.

The Brinad Parikrama and the Ramkoti Parikrama are led by ascetics only. Very few number of pilgrim participate in these two. The following customs are observed strictly by the ascetics and general pilgrim during Parikramas:

(1) Person of any caste, colour, sex or creed, abled or disabled can take part. No sense of hatred has been observed so far.
(2) Non-vegetarian dishes, alcohol and prohibited vegetables like onion and garlick are strictly discarded during the period.
(3) The whole Parikramas is done bare-footed.
(4) Pilgrims observe taboo on sexual intercourse during these days.
(5) The Ascetics avoid taking salt.

7

ASCETIC ORGANISATIONS AND THEIR PATRONAGE

The Vaishnava Ascetics Organisation i.e. Mutt/Sthan etc. discussed in the previous Chapter are somehow or other attached to any one of the existing three Vaishnava Systems — Dwara Gadi, Akhara and Khalas called hereby Patronage of Ascetic Organisations. Vaishnava Asceticism of present days have three peculiar systems as mentioned above. These three systems relate a Vaishnava ascetic with its spiritual heirarchy. In Dwara Gadi systems there are 52 (Fifty-two) Dwaras of Vaishnavas founded by great mystics of the sect. Vaishnava Ascetic Organisations can easily be linked with any of the Dwaras. The Akhara System was founded by one Baba Abhay Ram Das in 1720 A.D. at the time of Brindavan Kumbh. At present there are 18 Akhara of Vaishnava Ascetics. The Khalsa system is a latter development and it cannot be dated earlier than 1050 (one hundred and fifty) years form the present. They do not have their separate identity at the time of Kumbha but are attaching themselves with any one of the Akharas. At present they are Eight (8) in numbers.

The detailed study of all the three systems has been attempted in this Chapter under separate headings.

Dwara Gadi Systems of Vaishnava Ascetics

Vaishnavas have a peculiar Dwara Gadi System which relates one ascetic to its spiritual heirarchy of the family.

Almost all Vaishnava ascetics can tell their spiritual heirarchy These Dwaras are 52 (fifty-two) in numbers spread all over India. Ascetics belonging to a Dwara are Gurubhats (spiritual brothers) and members of the Gadi. All the ascetics, founder of the Dwara Gadies are believed to have been great mystics. The Dwaras are unifying forces among the Vaishnava Ascetics. One can easily link all the Vaishnava Mutta spread over different parts of India through the Dwara system. The table shows the distribution of Dwara Gadies all over India. Out of 52 (Fifty-two) Dwaras, 36 (Thirty-six) belong to Ramanand Sampraday, 10 (Ten) belong to Nimbark Sampradaya, 3 (Three) to Madhawa Sampradaya and 3 (Three) to Vishnuswami Sampradaya. A brief description of spiritual heirarchy of some of the Dwaras is given in the appendix and the table shows the places of Dwara with Acharya. Very recently the 36 (Thirty-six) Dwaras belonging to Ramanand Sampradaya have selected one over-all incharge of Ramanand Sampradaya and named him Sri Jagadguru Ramanandacharya.

Selection of Jagadguru Ramanandacharya

Like Shaivites, Ramanujites are also having the old tradition of selecting a Jagadguru Ramanujacharya. Till recently, the Ramanandies were accepting the leadership of Jagadguru Ramanujacharya, but in 1938 A.D. Swami Bhagwadacharya of Ayodhya declared himself as Jagadguru Ramanandacharya and bifurcated Ramanandies from Ramanujites. He could not receive the favour of all Ramanandies during his regime.

In the year 1977, at Allahabad Kumbha, all the Mahanths of 36 (Thirty-six) Ramanandi Dwaras collectively voted to have one Ramanandacharya and this way denied the supremacy of Ramanujites. In 1977 Kumbha three were three (3) contestants for the post, but Swami Sheo Ramacharya of Varanasi, Ramanand Pitha was unanimously voted to become Jagadguru Ramanandacharya. The Varanasi Sri Mutta has

List Showing the Dwaras of Vaishnavas Ramanand Sampradaya — 36 Dwaras

Sl. No.	*Gadyacharya*	*Guru of Gadyacharya*	*Gaddi*	*Place*
1.	Anantanand	Ramanand	Anant Gupta	Mathura
2.	Sursuranand	"	Sidhbaba Kijhadi	Aboo
3.	Narhariayanand	"	Gari Khala Sthan	Tanjeera
4.	Sukhanand	"	Shesabatika	Jaipur
5.	Ram Kabir	"	Kadam Kandi	Goverdhan
6.	Bhavanand	Ramanand	Shesabati	Churu (Fatehpur)
7.	Peepajee	Ramanand	Ramda (Peepakuti)	Bet Dwarika
8.	Yogananda	Ramanand	Ramkot (Gushnera)	Jaisalmer
9.	Abhayanand	Bhawanand	Chandpol Sri Balanand	Jaipur
10.	Keeljee	Krishnadasjee Paohari	Galtagaddi	Jaipur
11.	Agraswami	"	Revasa Shesabati	Jaipur
12.	Teelajee	"	Khandu Khandela	Karauli
13.	Bhagwatnarayan	"	Pindotaridham	Punjab
14.	Kewalkubajee	Narharidas	Jhinthda	Jodhpur
15.	Dadu Ram	Abhayanand	Ramitirth	Punjab
16.	Tantulsides	Tyagijee	Mudia Rampur	Barabanki
17.	Dev Murari	Tantulsidas	Daraganj	Prayag

18.	Mallookjee	Dev Murari	Kada Manikur	Prayag
19.	Dev Bhadanjee	Tantulsidas	Agrasthan	Itawa
20.	Hati Narayan	Krishnadas Paohari	Ashokur, Navada Shesabati	Jaipur
21.	Devakar	Agraswami	Jamal (Ghosa)	Jaipur
22.	Khojeejee	Gayasjee	Lahagarh	Jaipur
23.	Puran Vaivatee	Agrajee	Sarayasthan	Gwalior
24.	Lal Turangi	Krishnadas Panhari	Gurdaspur	Punjab
25.	Thambhanjee	Suryadas	Dadur Khan Kapid	Punjab
26.	Ram Rawaljee	Alhajee	Khodagaon	Jodhpur
27.	Ragochetan	Ramrawal	Bhandrej	Jodhpur
28.	Nabhajee	Agrajee	Gyanikasthan Gyansagar	Ajmer
`29.	Govinddas	Nabhajee	Rewalsar	Jaipur
30.	Karamchand	Anantanand	Dewasagram	Jaipur
31.	Kaloonayan	Purnavairati	Medgamkagram	Jodhpur
32.	Laha Rama	Teelajee	Khatu-Khandala	Jaipur
33.	Hanuman-Hathilejee	Agrajee	Mehdipur	Alwar
34.	Jangijee Tyagi	Agrajee	Patiyala	Punjab
35.	Alakhram	Yoganand	Hanuman Garhi (City)	Burma
36.	Ram Ramani	Khemdas	Medta	Jodhpur

Nimbark				
1.	Shobhu Ram	Harivyasdeo	Rudhiagram	Punjab
2.	Parasuramdeo	Harivyasadeo	Salemdbad	Ajmer
3.	Nagajee	Parmanand	Viharghat	Brindavan
4.	Viram Tyagi	Bhattjee	Krishnangarh	Kota
5.	Lafara Gopal	Harivyasadeo	Ghudala Gram	Rohtak
6.	Ghamand Deo	"	Kundalagram	Jodhpur
7.	Tatwaveta	Parasuramdeo	Jaitaran	Jodhpur
8.	Madhwadas	Harivyasadeo	Khanpur Karla	Kanil
9.	Chaturbhujdas	Hitharivansh	Hit Harivanshjee Ka Sthan	Brindavan
10.	Atma Ram	Sham Damodar	Maler Katta	Punjab
Madhwa				
1.	Krishnachaitanya	Vanimadhav Muni	Nadia Salimpur	Bengal
2.	Nityanand	"	"	"
3.	Shyamanand	Ballabhjee	Srinagarvat	Brindavan
Vishnuswami				
1.	Namdeo	Gyandeo	Pandarpur	Maharashtra
2.	Vithalnath	Ballabhacharya	Nathdwara	Udaipur
3.	Gokulnath	Vithalnath	Gokul	Mathura

(According to Sri Ram Taheldasjee)

been accepted as the Acharya Pitha of Ramanandies situated at Panch Ganga Ghat of Varanasi. Sri Ramanandacharya wore Ramraj coloured dress and carried one Dand on the top of which Sri Tingal mark is painted. This Dand is clad in a Saffron colour cloths. The present Ramanandacharya was adorned with the Dand on 12th February 1977 at his Gurusthan i.e. Ramanand Kote in Ahmedabad.

Akhara System Among Vaishnava Ascetics

Vaishnava Akharas were established in 1720 A.D. to defend Sanatan Dharma and Vaishnavism from foreign invaders who were against idol worship. In later period, it was strengthened and re-organised to defend Vaishnavas from Shaivas known as Sanyasin. This Akhara system was organised by the ascetics of northern India because Southern Ascetics were of individualistic opinion due to Alwar impact. So the followers of Ramanand felt need for defence and so united in one and the first organisation known as Ramdal formed under the leadership of Swami Balanand. This Ramdal helped Maharaja of Jaipur, Rajasthan in a battle and were inspired by the Maharaja to form a fighting force. There, at Maharaja's place they learned war tactics and the organisation came into foce with the financial help by Maharaja. At that very time they organised Chatuh Vaishnava Sampradaya into one militant force. The fulfledged organisational form came into force at the time of Brindavan Kumbha of 1720 A.D. At that time it was divided into three Anies known as Nirwani, Nirmohi and Digambari and Fifty-two Dwaras. These Anies were again sub-divided into Eight (8) Akharas and Eighteen sections — Chatuh Sampradaya includes Ramanandi, Madhwaites, Nimbarkism and Vishnuswamies. All the three Anies give equal importance to Rama and Krishna as the incarnation of Vishnu. In their correspondence they always write Sri Ram Krishnaya Namah (bow to Sri Ram and Krishna). At personal level in some Akharas Ram is given more importance, in other it is Krishna who matters greatly.

Out of the 16 (Sixteen) sections of Akharas, 5 (Five) are associated with Ram and 11 (Eleven) with Shyam (Krishna).

Nirmohi Ani	:	has three Akharas	
		(i)	Nirmohi
		(ii)	Mahanirwani
		(iii)	Santoshi
Digambari Ani	:	has to Akharas	
		(i)	Ramjee Digamber
		(ii)	Shyamjee Digamber
Nirwani Ani	:	has three Akharas	
		(i)	Nirwani
		(ii)	Khaki
		(iii)	Niravalambi

All these 8 (Eight) Akharas are again sub-divided into 18 (Eighteen) Sections as the list given below:

Nirmohi :	(i)	Ramanandi Nirmohi
	(ii)	Vishnuswami Nirmohi
	(iii)	Radhaballabh Nirmohi
	(iv)	Maladhari Nirmohi
	(v)	Jharia Nirmohi
Mahanirvani :	(i)	Ramanandi Mahanirwani
	(ii)	Harivyasi Mahanirvani
Santoshi :	(i)	Ramanandi Santoshi
	(ii)	Harivyasi Santoshi
Ramjee Digamber :	No Sections.	
Shyamjee Digamber		
Nirvani :	(i)	Ramanandi Nirvani
	(ii)	Harivyasi Nirvani
	(iii)	Balbhadri Nirvani
Khaki :	(i)	Ramanandi Khaki
	(ii)	Harivyasi Khaki
Niravalambi :	(i)	Ramanandi Niravalambi
	(ii)	Tatambari

Now-a-days Dadu Sampradaya has also formed at Akhara known as Dudhadhari Akhara with its principal seat at Narena. At the time of Kumbh they go for Sahi Snan (great bath) with Nirmohi Ani. Therefore Nirmohi Ani has five (5) and a half and this way the total comes to 16 (Sixteen) and half sections of Akharas.

Diagram Showing the Composition of the Vaishnava Akharas

A	B	C
1. Nirmohi		
	(i) Nirmohi	
		(a) Ramanandi Nirmohi
		(b) Bishnu Swami Nirmohi
		(c) Maladhari Nirmohi
		(d) Radhaballabh Nirmohi
		(e) Jharia Nirmohi
	(ii) Mahanirvani	(f) Ramanandi Mahanirvani
		(g) Harivyashi Mahanirvani
	(iii) Santoshi	(h) Ramanandi Santoshi
		(i) Harivyashi Santoshi
2. Digambari	(iv) Shyamjee Digamber	No Section
	(v) Ramjee Digamber	
3. Nirvani		
	(vi) Nirvani	
		(j) Ramanandi Nirvani
		(k) Harivyasi Nirvani
		(l) Balbhadri Nirvani
	(vi) Khaki	(m) Ramanandi Khaki
		(n) Harivyashi Khaki
	(vii) Niravalambi	(o) Ramanandi Niravalambi
		(p) Tatambari

A = ANI

B = AKHARA

C = SECTION OF THE AKHARA

On the basis of the data, enumerated, it can be said that including Dudhadhari Akhara. There are total sixteen and half Akharas among Vaishnavas at present.

Ghurye has described three Akharas in *Digambara Ani* including one 'Dhuriya-Digambara' as Akhara (Ghurye 1953, 181). Similarly Sinha and Saraswati have referred 'Ukhal Akhara' (Saraswati 1978,122). Even after deep enquiry these two Akharas as structural identity could not be located. The author was informed that 'Dhuriya Digambara' & 'Ukhal Akhara' are term of references used for the ascetics whose Akhara affiliation is not assertained by 'Kotwal' during examination of 'Taksar' (the codes of Akhara).

Membership of Akhara

The ascetic of Chathu Sampradaya, who is willing to serve the entire Sampradaya inspite of Gurusthan only, is taken into Akharas. He is called the Akharmal and also known as Rakmis (because he has taken vow to abide by the rules and regulations of Akhara). This Akharamalla is not bound by the rules of any one Gurusthan or Mutt. The Akharamalla lives with a Nagaatit for training and after initiation he is known as Sadik. He has to go through seven heirarchical stages for becoming a Nagaatit. These are as follows:

Ist Stage **Yatri**

The Chief duty of the Yatri is to collect tooth stick for the superior ascetics and to wonder about the places of pilgrimage either alone or with Jamat.

IInd Stage **Chhora**

To serve his superior in various ways such as drawing water, preparing the leaf chips and plates etc.

IIIrd Stage **Bandagidar**

To look after the stores and cooking, to bring dishes for

offerings. Cleaning the temple and utensils of Naga Atit and in his leisure to study under the guidance of Guru.

IVth Stage **Hurdanga**

To cook the food, to bring the dishes for offerings to deity, call Harihar, to carry the insignia and flag of Akhara, and to master the use of weapons are his duties.

Vth Stage **Murethiya**

To worship deities, to call Jai, to supervise the works of Sevaks and to be well-experienced in the sue of weapons are the main duties of Murethiya.

VIth Stage **Naga**

To administer the Akhara, to worship the deity, to protect the properties of Akhara and the Mutts of Sampradaya, to lead the Jamat to various places, to make preparations for the Kumbha, and to propagate Vaishnavism are the duties of a Naga. It takes twelve (12) years' time to become a Naga.

VIIth Stage **Atita**

To consider the important issues of the Sampradayas and to solve them, to guide the Nagas in matters considering their spiritual well-being, and to remain absorbed in worship are the responsibilities of the Atita. The Atitas are believed to be the Siddha Nagas (The Nagas with miraculous power).

When an ascetic becomes a Naga then he is known as Punch of Akhara and they enjoy the right to vote and work for Akhara.

Sadar Naga

The Sadar Naga title is bestowed on the individual after 12 (Twelve) years. Before Kumbha a day is fixed for the function which is called Rakam Kadin (day of Rakam). This is the most auspicious day in the life of an ascetic where Panchan bestow the title. At this time Naga is taught the

Rakam which is the principle secret of the Organisation. This is known as:

(a) Do Rakam Kadari
(b) Do Rakam Sadri

On Jajam (the gathering of Panchan), the Panchas presents Kanthi, cup and service of ascetic called Kotwal to the Sadar Naga. Soon after his selection he forms a Jamat with whom he wanders away form place to place for 12 (Twelve) years. In course of his tour he is required to increase the number of Vaishnavas and propagates Vaishnavaism and to collect money for Akhara. Besides these, he has to look after the general welfare of the Akhara and its members.

All the Six (6) Stages described above are of Three (3) years each and Sadar Naga for 12 (Twelve) years and Atit is the honour for life. The ascetic of the highest order is known as Maha Atit and performs all such functions worthy of him.

For administrative control 52 (Fifty-two) Mahanths are kept under one Sadar Naga and 52 (Fifty-two) Nagas are put under one Atit. The decision of these two are final and binding over all the Fifty-two (52) Mahanths and Nagas. One day of Rakam or Nagotswa, Nagas are provided with Sellies (a rope of black colour) the Selly is made up of Seri-thread of black colour which is being worn by the Nagas as per the following order:

Nagas of Nirmohi Ani wears the Selly in the right leg, Nagas of Nirwani Ani wears it in the left leg, Nagas of Digamber Ani do not wear the Selly but they always keep it with them with due honour. The Nirwani Ani has four Sellies — Sagaria, Basantia, Haridwari and Ujjania.

There is a fixed rule for making the Latoory (matted hair) and putting the Sindur (sandal) known as Mahabiri.

Mahabiri : Ascetics of Nirmohi Ani put on the Mahabiri at the right eye-brow. The Digambars put on in the middle of the eye-brows and the Nirvanis put on at the left eye-brow.

Latoory : The Latoory of Nirmohies hangs on the right side of the head of Digambar in the middle of the head and of Nirvani it is on the left side of the head.

Nishan — Insignia or Flag of Akharas

All the Akharas are having their Nishan. The Nishan of five Akharas, worshippers of Ram contains the mark of Hanuman with a sun mark in left side.

The Nishan of eleven Akharas — worshipers of Shyam contains the mark of Hanuman with Garuda (Monstrous eagle) mark in the right. Colour of the Nishan differs from Ani to Ani as per follows:

Digamber	:	Panchranga (Five coloured)
Nirmohi	:	Shining green
Nirwani	:	Golden

Tradition for Calling Jai in the Akhara

The ascetics of every Akhara before starting any good work call a Jai as per tradition:

(1) Charo Sampradayaon Ki Jai
(2) Bawan Dwaron Ki Jai
(3) Anant Koti Vaishnava Ki Jai
(4) Apne Guru Ki Jai
(5) Hanuman and Garuda Deo Ki Jai
(6) Sri Ram Krishna Deo Ki Jai
(7) Sri Maha Prasad Ki Jai
Jai - Jai Sita Ram
Jai - Jai Radheshyam

All the Anies and Akharas have their principal seats or Baithakas as the gravitational points in their wonderings and pilgrimages. Following is the distribution of their Baithaks":

Nirwani Ani :	Ayodhya (Hanuman Garhi), Chitrakut, Ujjain, Puri, Goverdhan and Nasik.
Digambari :	Ayodhya, Chitrakut, Nasik, Ujjain, Vrindavan, Puri.
Nirmohi :	Ayodhya, Vrindavan, Chitrakut, Nasik, Ujjain, Puri, Goverdhan, Bundi, Kota.

Ani Mahanth

By consensus of all, one Sri Mahanth and one Prime Minister are elected who controls the Sahi Snan (kingly bath) of Kumbha. At present Baba Ram Khelawan Das, Singhatha Kesri of Nirwani Akhara is Rii Mahanth of Ani, 86 (Eighty-six) years Maha-Atit.

Sri Panch Ramanandiya Nirwani Akhara

Nirwani Akhara has Hanuman Garhi, Ayodhya, as Centre. The detialed study including history, administrative organisation, judicial organisation and rules and regulations etc. are being dealt herewith.

History of Hanuman Garhi

It is believed that King Vikramaditya-II constructed one palace of Kasauti stone (black) at Janmabhumi. From that time the Hanuman Kote area is being called Hanuman Garhi. At the end of Fifth Century A.D., Sanyasis captured the Garhi and they worshipped the idol of Hanuman by the name of Bhairava. Then the Mohammadans came and worshipped the idol by the name of Hathile Sahab. In the beginning of Eighteenth Century Vikram, the Head of Nirwani Akhara, Baba Abhayram captured the Garhi from Mohammadam. This news reached to the Nawab of Awadh at Lucknow who sent his military to help the Muhammadans but the Khatriyas of Banswara defeated them. Then the Badsah of Delhi sent a bigger army which came to Ayodhya. The Talukdars of Barabanki, Pratapgarh Sultanpur, Bahraiach, Gonda and Faizabad fought unitedly aganist the Delhi army and defeated them. In the mean time Baba Abhayram called all the followers of his Sampradaya form Haridwar, Ujjain, Nasik and Ganga Sagar and established a trained army. In the mean time Nawab Mansur Ali Khan fell seriously ill and came to Baba Abhay Ram who gave him Bhibhooti (the sacred ash) and his illness recovered. The Nawab sanctioned a Maffee of Eight (8) villages to Baba Abhay Ram after consultation with Raja Mansingh, his adviser and Tikait Ray, his Minister. He also ordered his Minister Tikait Ray to construct a fortess on Hanuman Kila, which was known as Hanuman Garhi. In this way the present fortess (temple) came into existence, at the time of Baba Abhayram in the year 1960 A.D. In the year 1855 A.D. the Hindu and Mohammadans fought for this temple. At that time, the King of Ayodhya Maharaja Man Singh, Kayamjang, defended the fortees with his military power. Again a few years later Maulabi Amir Ali of Amethi wanted to capture the Garhi in the name of Islam. The British President passed on order to check it to Wajeed Ali Sah who checked Amir Ali for doing so. Then he sent his Wajeer, Mirja Ali Khan Bahadur to investigate the case and then gave his verdict in favour of Hindus. The Maulvi Amir Ali disobeyed the order and declared war. By the order of King of Lucknow Mr. Barolo came with his army to check Amri Ali. They fought the war but Amir Ali took lead. Then the Talukdar of Raja Sher Bahadur Singh came with his army and killed Maulabi Amir Ali in the battle. This incident is written in Atikhe Ayodhya by Ram Durga Prasad Singh the Magistrate of Sadila.

From that very time the Hanuman Garhi is under the disciples of Abhayram Das who was the Gaddinasain Mahanth. After him the other Mahanths were:

Jagannath Das
Gopal Das
Mangal Das
Awadhram Das
Balram Das
Bhagwan Das (3.1.1867)
Balak Das (30.6.1867)
Lakshman Das (17.12.1872)
Hanuman Das (13.12.1890)
Bhagat Ram Das (14.3.1899)
Jagannath Das (23.1.1908)
Shyam Sundar Das (20.12.1909)
Harnarayan Das (23.3.1917)
Sitaram Das (5.1.1941)
Ram Das (20.8.1978)
Ram Balak Das (present)

Administrative Organisation

The organisation has unique Panchayaty-System. Nearly 500-600 Ascetics — Naga, Atit, the followers of Ramanand Sampradaya mainly Virakt — Vaishnava are residing. It has a temple with Hanuman (the Monkey God) as principal deity. The working of Mahanth, rights and duties, appointments are done under a special rule. The appointment of Mahanth is based on the decision of Panchan Akhara and not on Guru-Chela tradition, Panchan Pith selects the Mahanths of all the four branches, as also of the rules and regulations that govern them.

The Mahanths of all the Pattis have enhanced the property and their main temple of Hanuman. The management of the temple, the customs of Akhara, the appointment of Mahanth and Pujari and the rights and duties of Panchan are governed by a special tradition described in foregoing pages of this Chapter.

During the time of Mahanth Balram Das, the administration of Garhi was set up on a democratic basis. Four brnaches of Akhara—Patti Haridwari, Patti Basantiya, Patti Ujjainiya and Patti Sagriya were established with different Mahanths for each Patti. The property and Chattal of the Akhara was distributed among four Pattis best officially, since then this Akhara is continuing at the same place. After some time each Patti was further divided into three parts called Jammat-Jammat Khalsa, Jammat Dunda and Jammat Jhundi. Under each Jammat, two Thoks were set up, where the Aasan of the ascetics of Akhara were established. Being a Panchayati Matta, the office rights and entries of Naga and Atti Sadhus are equal. They have equal opportunities for the Chief Post, and chances of strike are very dim. The present administrative heirarchy is shown by Chart-1, 2 and 3. Mahanth Gaddinashin is the Chief of the Organisation. Under his command there are four Pattis with Four (4) Mahanths as Chief of Four (4) Patties. Then each Patti have one Mukhatar, one Pujari, one Kothari, Three Golkies, Twelve Panch and a number of Sadhus.

Gaddinashin

Sagariya Patti | Ujjainia Patti | Haridwari Patti | Basantia Patti

(under Haridwari Patti:) Jammat-I | Jammat-II (Dunda) | Jammat-III

(under Jammat-II (Dunda):) Thok-I | Thok-II

(under Thok-I:) Asan | Asan | Asan | Asan

(Chart-I—Showing Organisation of the Garhi)

Gaddinashin

Mahanth | Mahanth | Mahanth | Mahanth

Mahanth
Mukhtar-I
Pujari-I
Kothari-I
Golki-3
Panch-12
Variances 100 to 200

(Chart-II—Showing the official heirarchy of the PATTI)

Gaddinashin

(Baba Ram Balak Dasjee)

Sl. No.	*Appoint-ments*	*Sagaria Patti*	*Ujjainia Patti*	*Basantiya Patti*	*Haridwari Patti*
1.	Mahanth	Sri Ram Kishun Dasjee	Sri Chhatradhari Dasjee	Sri Narayan Dasjee (Bulbulia Baba)	Sri Ram Sewak Dasjee
2.	Kothari	Sri Rajinder Dasjee	Sri Balu Ram Bharosha Dasjee	Sri Murli Dasjee	Sri Ram Sharan Dasjee (Neta)
3.	Mukhtar	Sri Lal Babu	Sri Radha Babu	Sri Shamsher Bahadur	Sri Triveni Lal

(Chart-III—Showing the names of appointments at present in the Garhi)

Rules of Akhara

A Sadhu of Chhatuh Sampradaya willing to serve the Sampradaya mere than his Gurusthan can be it's member. The Sadhu that obeys the rules and regulations of Akhara is known as Akharamalla. This is the first stage of recruitment. After passing through various stages described earlier, becomes Naga. He is known as Sadhik of the Akhara. In this stage be forms his own group of Sadhus called Jamaat and allowed to move outside with his group but he remains part and parcel of Akhara. Any Vaishnava Sadhu, who is the disciple of Naga-Atti of Hanuman Garhi is entitled to the membership of Akhara, and is called Sadik-Chela of his Guru. Sadhus are given a share of the food from the Akhara after fifteen days of initiation. A Sanskrit School has been established to educate such new Sadhu and it is the duty of their Sidh-Guru to familiaries with the cusotms of Akhara. The Sadhus are bestowed with the title of Naga after they have achieved all other grades Chela to Murethia. A ceremony for this purpose is held on the Chadao of Kumbha and is called Nagotsava. Such ceremonies are also held in the Hanuman Garhi itself.

There are three (3) types of Panchayat in the Akhara. They are:

(i) Patti Panchayat
(ii) Akhara Panchayat
(iii) Panchayat of Akhara Executive

(i) Patti Panchayat

The Sadhus of all the three Jamaats of a Patti are the members of this Panchayat and are called Panchan of Patti. They are responsible for the property of the Patti, and solves the disputes by majority or consensus. They also select, appoint or suspend the Mahanth of a Patti. If any Sadhu or Mahanth acts against the prestige of the Matt or his Iqrarnama , he can be warned, fined or even expelled from Patti by this Panchayat. Usually, the Mahanth is the Chairman of Panchayat.

(ii) Akhara Panchayat

The Sadhus and Naga-Arits of all the four Pattis are the members of this Panchayat. It has the duty to look after the property of Akhara and Chhaumali. This Panchayat elects Mahanth Gaddinashin and the members of executive committee. It decides all the matters pertaining to the Akhara and also about any complaints of any sort about a Sadhu.

Every year in the month of Kartik, an account of expenses is presented to the Panchayat who passes it after the due consideration the Mahanth-Gaddinashin is the Chairman of this Panchayat.

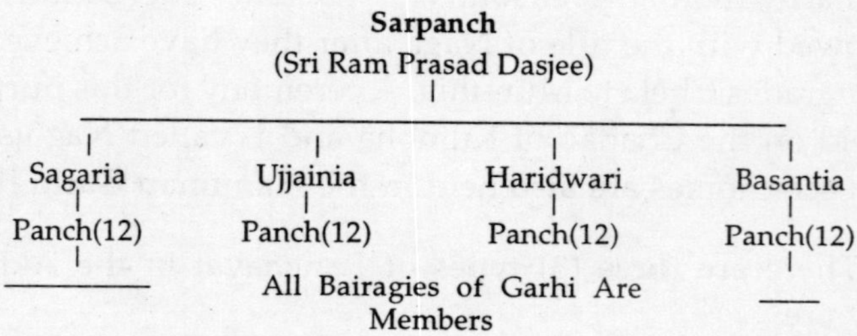

(Fig. IV: Showing Judicial Organisation of Hanuman Garhi).

List of Panchan

Sl. No.	*Name*	*Guru's name*	*Patti*	*Jamaat*	*Desig-nation*
1.	Baba Pandiṭ Ram Prasad Das	Ram Prasad Dass	Ujjainia	—	Sarpanch
2.	Baba Sarju Das	Ram Lochan Das	"	Dunda	Panch
3.	Ramphal Das	Ram Karan Das	"	"	"
4.	Abhiram Das	Sarju Das (Sadhakcha)	"	Khalsa	"
5.	Sarju Das	Sheo Ram Das	"	"	"
6.	Ram Piyare Das	Ram Das	"	Jhundi	"
7.	Siya Ram Das	Raghunath Das	"	"	"
8.	Ram Bharora Das	Dharm Das	Haridwari	Dunda	"
9.	Trivani Das	Ram Ratan Das	"	"	"
10.	Awadh Bihari Das	Chandrabali Das	"	Jhundi	"
11.	Ram Rup Das	Jamuna Das	Haridwari	Jhundi	Panch
12.	Muneshwar Das	Deo Narayan Das	"	Khalsa	"
13.	Chhabile Das	Govind Das	"	"	"
14.	Ram Deo Das	Amant Das	Sagaria	Dunda	"
15.	Ram Narayan Das	Raghunath Das	"	"	"
16.	Ram Sarup Das	Raghunath Das	"	Khalsa	"
17.	Ram Kishore Das	Chandam Das	"	"	"

18. Jagganath Das	Bhagwan Das	"	Jhundi	"
19. Ram Balak Das	Jamuna Das	"	"	"
20. Ram Das	Shyam Sunder Das	Basantia	Dunda	"
21. Din Bandhu Das	Balram Das	"	"	"
22. Sarju Das	Teja Das	"	Khalsa	"
23. Ram Samp Das	Ganga Das	"	"	"
24. Ram Charita Das	Ram Sanigh Das	"	Jhundi	"
25. Bhola Das	Parmeshwar Das	"	"	"

These members the elect a Sarpanch (shown in the Chart-IV)

This Panchayat is headed by the Sarpanch and has a life of two years. Sarpanch convenes the meetings and gives his ruling and permission for voting on a subject. Each member has to take an oath of honesty and truthfulness in front of Sarpanch. Sarpanch himself takes this oath in front of Mahanth-Gaddinashin.

Ten (10) or more members can requisition a meeting of the Panchayat in writing, the quorum of Executive Panchayat is 16 (sixteen). Usually it considers any matter which could not be decided by the Patti or Akhara Panchayat, or if a member is not satisfied by the decision of those Panchayat. Formerly, a consensus was necessary for a decision, but now a majority is sufficient. Sarpanch can cast his decisive vote in case of a dead-lock.

The Sarpanch or any Panch can be removed from his office only when he dies, or resigns or is impeached. The decision of this Panchayat is final and binding and has to be accepted by all the Sadhus of Akhara.

The Executive Panchayat was set up to protect the customs and traditions of the Akhara, its fame and honour and to properly manage the Hanuman Garhi.

Rights of Executive Panchayat

If there is any complaint of breaking of tradition,

favouritism, financial irregularities and meddling in the affairs of other Pattis against any Sadhus the Panchayat, by way of punishment first of all warns him. If he repeats the act he is fined to the tune of Rs. 200/- (Rupees two hundred) and if his crimes recur, he may be fined more than Rs. 200/-.

If any Sadhu disobeys the rulings and traditions of Panchayat and Akhara, he may be asked to vacate the Asan or even expelled from the Garhi. The Sarpanch or a member of the Panchayat can be expelled from the Panchayat in case of absence without any proper reason for three consecutive meetings.

Rules Governing the meeting of Akhara

(a) A Kotwal is appointed, who is responsible for the meeting of Patti, Akhara and executive Panchayat. It is his duty to inform every Asan of the time and venue of meeting.

(b) When a meting is called, those members who are present in the Garhi can reach a decision even if some members are out on Ramnat or Jamaat. Their decision is taken for the decision of whole Akhara or Patti.

(c) The decision of Panchayat can be given to any Sadhu in writing by way of certificate which is signed by all the present members. This is called Panchanama.

(d) Voting, if necessary, is done by raising hands. In case of dead-lock, the Chairman caste the final vote.

(e) If a Sadhu, or Sadhus, against whom a decision has been reached fails to be present in the meeting, he or they are informed by the Chairman of the decision. He has no right to overlook this decision.

The Garhi is headed by the Mahanth-Gaddinashin, who for all practical purposes, is just a manager of the Garhi, despite the fact that every property of the Garhi is registered in his name. The Panchan are the real owners.

Selection of Mahanth Gaddinashin

The Mahanth is elected by the Akhara Panchayat. The Mahanths are elected from each Pattis by rotation. The Panchan of the rest three(3) Pattis take part in election, and decision is reached by majority, if consensus fails.

Rules Governing Mahanth Gaddinashin

The Mahanth cannot go out of the four walls of Garhi. He may go out on express approval of Akhara Panchan only for festivals. He can then go out with ceremony. In all official matters Mukhtareama represents him. The Gaddinashin is taken for both the Chief Manager and Sewait (Servant) of the Garhi. His Gaddi is just in front of Hanuman temple.

Before assuming office, the Mahanth designate, has to execute an Iqararnama which is —

- Agree to abide by customs and traditions of Garhi.
- Never act against the Dharma.
- Shall act with the advise of Akhara Panchan.
- Shall not claim any share in the property donated to the Garhi during his tenure.
- Shall have no right to transfer the property registered in his name.
- If the Panchayat ever receive any complaints against him, he can be removed.

Then he is given the garland of Mahanth and this ceremony is announced by Knoll. The Mahanth is responsible to the Akhara Panchayat and it is his duty to present the balance sheet of expenses to the Panchayat.

Selection of the Patti-Mahanth

(a) The Patti Mahanth is selected from each Jamaat in

rotation. The Jamaat from which the Mahanth is to be elected does not take part in the selection, only other two Jamaats take part.

(b) Mahanth is elected by majority of the Panchas of the two Jamaats.

(c) He, too, has to execute an Iqararnama on the same lines as Mahanth Gaddinashin.

This election is also announced by the Knolls of Patti. Details of organisational chart of a Patti is given in chart II.

Right of Purjarpana of Temple

The income from the Hanuman Garhi temple is called Pujarpana. The rights of priest-hood are as follows:

(a) Each Patti is represented by one priest in the temple.

(b) The term of priest is six months or one year.

(c) The term of Pujarpana—

Patti Haridwari and Sagaria	:	From Chaitra to Phalgun
Patti Basantia	:	From Kunwar to Bhadrapada
Patti Ujjainia	:	Agrahun Badi Panchami to Chaitra.

(d) Rights of priest-hood is to the three Jamaats of Patti, the two Thoks of each Jamaat and then the Asans. Some times, the two Thoks have been awarded Six (6) months each. But in Patti Basantia, in Jamaat Jhundi, the right of Thok Paramhans Rameshwar Das is 75 per cent and that of Thok Swami Sryudas is 25 per cent. When the term of priest-hood is of any Thok each Asan get the rights for 6 (Six) months. The end of first Six (6) months is called Mela Chaiti and the second half is called Mela Kartiki.

(e) Each Naga under an Asan gets equal opportunity by rotation. They are selected by the Jamaat Panchan or Patti Panchan.

(f) Usually the selections are made a month before, the new term begins. If unsatisfied by the decision, a Naga can go upto Akhara Panchayat whose decision is final and binding.

(g) A Naga can assume priest-hood only if he pays outstanding sum due to him from Akhara or Patti.

(h) The selected priest has to deposit a fixed sum (Rs. 660/- only) then he is given right of admission into the temple by the Panchan or Mahanth.

(i) If a new priest does not know the ways of worshipping, he is taught before assuming office.

(j) The Mukhtare-Am on behalf of the Mahanth Gaddinashin officially relieves the outgoing priest and gives charge to the new one, in writing.

(k) The incumbent will remain priest unless — he dies or

— Becomes physically unfit

— declared unfit by the Panchan

— expelled from the Garhi.

If it happens, the next Naga will take over, belong to the same Asan.

(l) Only a Sutradhari can become a priest. If it is the turn of a Maladhari he can send a Sutradhari on his behalf.

(m) The income from the temple is used for other Akhara purposes also.

(i) Arrangements of worshipping, offerings and festivals;

(ii) The expenses for sweeping, white washing and repairing of temple;

(iii) Daily Sidha to each Sadhu of his Patti;

(iv) Wages for the servants of Cow-Sheds and Akhara;

(v) Expenses for the Sadhus of Patti;

(vi) Special foods to each Sadhus on special occasions;

(vii) For expenses (monthly), fruits on Ekadasi days,

(viii) Equal distribution of the balance money between the four Pattis;

(ix) Purchase of any temple article.

Rights of Property

A Sadhu is the owner of all his properties and belongings. In case there is no successor, his property will be attached to the Patti.

Taboos on Sadhus

The Sadhus are Nihang i.e. they cannot marry nor have sexual relation with any woman. It is understood that if this happens that Sadhu shall voluntarily break-off the relations with Garhi. In case of default, the Panchayat can take proper action.

Economy

A Mukhtar is appointed to keep an account of the expenses, and a Golki as the cashier. These two have all the economic responsibilities. The latter are selected form each Jamaat for three years. The Mukhtars are hereditory.

Each Patti has its own Mukhtar too, who are Kayastha by caste. Thus, the economy of Akhara is managed by Mahanth Gaddinashin, Mukhtar and Golki.

Branches of Garhi

Its one branch has been established in Gangasagar, West

Bengal which has an imposing status of Kapil Muni. A Mela is held on the occasion of Makar Sankranti. This place is also governed on the lines of Hanuman Garhi.

In addition, there are other branches at Ujjain, Brindavan, Nasik, Haridwar, Prayag, Jagannath Puri, Surajkund, Faizabad etc. These all are managed by Hanuman Garhi.

Important Festivals of Hanuman Garhi

Following festivals are celebrated on large scale by the ascetics of Garhi:

(i)	Hanumat Jayanti	:	Kartik Krishna Paksha Fourteenth day.
(ii)	Rangbhari Ekadasi	:	Falgun Sukla Paksha Eleventh day.
(iii)	Full Bangla	:	Asharh Sukla Paksha.
(iv)	Dashara	:	Nishan of all Akharas starts from Hanuman Garhi.
(v)	Parikrama	:	Kartik Sukla Paksha Eleventh Day.

Public Works

(1) Sanskrit Mahavidyalaya is run by Garhi which was given donation of Rs. 1,00,000/- (Rupees one Lakh only). It is affiliated to Varanaseya Sanskrit Viswavidyalaya. Having a building of Ten (10) rooms, education is upto Acharya i.e. M.A.

(2) Gosala : One huge Gosala where cattles are given food.

(3) Vyayamshala : There is a famous wrestling centre with wrestlers, of repute like Baba Haridasjee (Hindkesari/Sitare Hind), Baba Sukhram Dasjee,

Ramsewak Dasjee and Gyan Dasjee.

(4) Dharmsala : One Dharmasala for the welfare and stay of Pilgrims being run by the Garhi.

Other Akharas and their Place at Ayodhya

Digamber Akhara

This Akhara was organised under Sri Balram Das nearly Two hundred (200) years ago. The present Mahanth Pratiwadi Bhayanker—Paramhansa Ramchandra Dasjeeis is Eleventh in the spiritual hierarchy. In the year 1905 as per Awadh Gazzateer only Twenty-five (25) Sadhus were residing in the Palace. At present only Eight (8) persons belonging to places like Bihar, Uttar Pradesh and Rajasthan are residing there. The present Mahanth is a learned man and very keen participant in politics. He was also Ward Chairman of Faizabad Municipality. He finally associated with National Politics supporting Jana Sangh now Bhartiya Janata Party and Bharat Sadhu Samaj.

Present Organisation

Mahanth

(Sri Paramhans Ramchandra Das)

|

Pujari (2)

|

Kothari (1)

|

Bhandari (3)

This Organisation is having agricultural land in three villages of Uttar Pradesh as the source of main income.

Ramanandi Khaki Akhara

At the time of Nawab Sirajudaullah, Sadhu Dharamdasjee

of Chitrakut founded the present Baithak at Ayodhya. At present Ram Ratan Dasjee is Thirteenth (13th) Mahanth on spiritual heirarchy. This Organisation has a huge building with a temple having tutelary deity Ram-Parivar. Only four persons are living inside the Mutt. All other Sadhus believed to be one hundred in numbers are busy in agricultural work in the Basti district of Uttar Pradesh. The rooms of the Mutt are given on lease to local persons. Mahanthjee is entirely looking for agricultural work. The Pujari is a Bhajanandi Sadhu and he is unable to give details about Sthan.

Nirmohi Akhara

The founder of this place of Akhara was Mahatma Govind Das of Jaipur. He established the present Mutt in Ramkot area of Ayodhya. The present Mahanth is ninth in heirarchy.

Niravalambi Akhara

Mahatma Virmalladasjee of Kota, Rajasthan founded this Baithak. The present Mahanth is Sri Narsingh Dasjee.

Santoshi Akhara

The founder of this Baithaka was Sri Rati Ram Dasjee of Jaipur. The present building was reconstructed by Radha Krishna Dasjee. After his death in 1920 A.D. the place is vacant still.

Mahanirwani Akhara

The present Baithak was founded by Purussotham Dasjee of Bundi at the time of Nawab Siraijuddaullah. At present the Seventh (7th) Mahanth is on the seat. Nearly Twenty-five (25) ascetics are residing in the Baithaka at present.

Khalsa System Among Vaishnava Ascetics

In Chhatuh-Sampradaya Vaishnava the Khalsa system is a later origin than Akharas. It may be after the influence of Sikkism, but no evidence of their impact is available. This

Khalsa system is founded nearly One hundred and Fifty years (150) years B.P., of Militant Vairagies known as Chhatuh Sampradaya Khalsa. Upto the recent Kumbha-Parva these Khalsas have not made their separate identity at the time of Sahistnan, but they are being attached with any one of the Akharas specially with Digamber. At present there are eight Khalsas — as follows:

Chhatuh-Sampradaya-Khalsa

Dakore	Dadia (Barah-bhai)	Tyagi (Terah-bhai)	Kanpur	Ayodhya	Itawa	Mahat-yagi	Saptri-shi & Sankadik

The first Khalsa was founded by Baba Mangaldasjee approximately 150 (One hundred and Fifty) years ago. This Khalsa was called Dakore Khalsa. It is because the founder's place was Dakor village. His follower Baba Nandilab Dasjee when developed his disciples, established a new settlement and called it Barah Bhai Dadia. After him Sri Mahanth Dharamdasjee took the charge. Baba Jaggannathdasjee of Jaggannath Puri started capturing the Ganj (store of food-grains) his Adhikari Baba Damodar Dasjee started initiating disciples and established a strong Dadia Khalsa.

At the time of one Ujjain Kumbh Baba Narsighdasjee established a new Ganj (store and sit), at the Mangal Ghat. Baba Ragubir Dasjee of Kanpur also established a Ganj at the same time, and called themselves Tyagi Khalsa and in both, one Mahanth Siyaramdasjee was nominated as Sri Mahanth of newly formed Tyagi Khalsa. After him Baba Arjundasjee took the charge. After a lapse of years Tyagi Khalsa divided into two Mahatyagi headed by Sri Baldeodasjee and Saptarishi or Sanakadik headed by Sri Sheetaldasjee upto two generations i.e. Sri Ram Jeevan Dasjee and Sri Prayag Dasjee both were working together. Due to some differences Baba Ram Sukh

Dasjee separated themselves and put the Mahatyagis in one separate group. Again the Saptarishi Khalsa was divided into seven groups headed by different individuals and these individuals organised their separate units. These units are known after the establishers' name e.g. Nakchheda Narayan Das, Badmuchha Narayan Das etc.

The Dadia Khalsa was divided into three major groups, Kanpur, Ayodhya and Itawa. Kanpur-Khalsa was established by Sri Raghubirdasjee at Kanpur followed by Haigriva Dasjee and present Mahanth is Ramdasjee. Ayodhya-Khalsa by Bhaktmali Ram Saran Dasjee known as Bhakt Mali Mandir. Itawa-Khalsa was organised by Sri Brindaban Dasjee at Itawa and he is the ruling Mahanth.

The Khalsas do not have any established code of conduct like Akharas but one thing is common i.e. keeping the matted hair and wearing the ashes known as Panchadhuani Bhasm. The Tyagis, some of them wear only Langot of banana skin and some wear Achala and copeen of cloths.

At Ayodhya there are four Muttas of Khalsas:

1.	Terahbhai Tyagi Khalsa	:	Khakchauk, Nayaghat
2.	Barah Bhai Dadia	:	Jânki Chat
3.	Ayodhya Khalsa	:	Bhaktmali Mandir, Ramghat
4.	Dakor Khalsa	:	Raghawjee Ka Mandir, Ramghat.

8

INTERACTION BETWEEN ASCETICS AND HOUSE-HOLDERS

Among Anthropologists, Oliver (referred by Romney, 1961, 223) has discussed the concept of inter-action in detail. According to him:

> All interactions may be viewed as having duration and discernible sequence of action, and it has always been described in terms of the spacial arrangements between the interacters. Also native terms of reference, if not of address, usually exist to describe the interactor's role in the events under consideration. Moreover, it is probably rare for emotion to be entirely absent in interaction, on the other hand, transactions, as we define this dimension of interaction, do not necessarily accompany all interactions (quoted by Romney, 1961, 223).

The concept has other views too. It can be viewed as an interactive situation between individuals when they influence one another. In this Chapter, I have dealt with the interaction of ascetics on inter and inter-group levels. Inter-group include interaction between ascetics and Mahanth, Guru-Shishya, between two organisations, between two Mahants and intra-group includes ascetics and house-holders.

Interaction Between Guru and Shishya

This is commonly called Guru-Shishya Relation. Classical texts in India have attached much importance to Diksha. While explaining its importance it is said that initiation is compulsory for a Hindu because no religious ritual bears any fruit unless a man is initiated by a Guru. It has been elaborately explained that even a minor good action of an initiated person gives fruitful results while great religious rituals even become fruitless of an un-initiated one. It is also said that initiation is essential for getting Sadgati, after death. Although the general maxim prescribes salvation after death at Kashi or at Ayodhya. The texts also say that even Shiva or Vishnu initiate the person who dies uninitiated at Kashi or Ayodhya.

Whatever may lie the reason or idea behind all these opinions may be accepted without any doubt that a Guru enjoys a very high position in Hindu society due to his knowledge, spirituality and lofty actions. The word itself explains that a Guru is one who drives away the darkness of his disciples. It means that a Guru is thought to have himself realised the truth and have made his life superior than general mass. Due to his talent the Guru occupied a very respectable position and people approached him for peace and prosperity and also for enlightenment. The Guru is directly communicable like the God, and grants immediate relief. He listens, answers and helps in solving the problems at once by miracle or by grace or by dialectical skill. With the blessings of Guru the Shishya become free from dangers and attains everything as desired by him. The kind and the degree depends upon the nature of faith and behaviour thereby. The Shishya also is supposed to follow the directions of his Guru abstaining himself from any kind of evil desire or action.

In this way the relationship between Guru and Shishya is very remarkable. Acharya Deo Bhava goes to direct people who consider Guru as God. The moment a person is taken into asceticism, is being initiated by his ascetic Guru and is required to abide by the rules laid down by the Guru. This relation among the ascetics is like father and son. In general practice it is written like Ram Das Chela Hari Das it is in place of writings like Baburam son of Sita Ram. In course of introduction, in the writing for heirarchy Guru's name is used in place of father's name. The ascetics of Gurus order are called Kaka-Guru. The Guru's Guru is called Dada-Guru etc. The Shishya shows due respect and humble submission to Guru. Whenever any suspicious occasion comes he invites his Guru giving him first and foremost position. He also offers first regard to his Guru at the time of daily Puja. Keeps photo or any belongings of his Guru with him and offers flowers and prayers to him. He keeps himself away from criticism of Guru and also his criticizers. He attains the functions of the Guru-Gaddi, specially at the time of Guru-Purnima all the ascetics Shishya gather at Guru-Gaddi to offer prayers to him.

The Guru also keeps an eye on the Shishya, makes necessary religio-spiritual arrangements for the welfare of Shishya, and gives necessary directions from time to time. While for a Shishya it is essential to visit the Guru-Gaddi, it is the Gurukripa only that takes a Guru to the place of Shishya. Spiritually speaking, an able Guru infuses his power to a faithful Shishya and makes him a man of good ideas and actions. Shishya puts on the Tilak Mark of his Gurusthan only. This also works as an identification mark. Two ascetic Shishya of the same Guru are called Guru-Bhais. The ascetic initiated first will be the elder one.

Interaction Between Organisations

In spite of diversities India is famous for its initial unity and this phenomenon is found in every walk of life. This is more prominent in ascetic life. Though there are different cults in asceticism like Shaiva, Vaishnava, Shakta and also different sub-cults in Vaishnavism like Ramanuj, Ramanand, Nimbark etc. They are basically united because the Vedic texts have already established the fact of oneness, of God. The different ascetic organisations have the same ideal of the greatest good to the greatest number. At Ayodhya, some Organisations are of Ramanujites, some are of Ramanandies, some are of Udasins. They have their different daily routine, different mode of worship but they all agree in as much as they aim at forming religious surroundings with a view to spread Ram Bhakti and to train the general public in Ram Charita. From time to time they organise general meetings for explaining their views and mutual discourses. Whenever any complication arises in a particular organisation, (not of homely character) other organisations come to its help and in this way their mutual relationship strengthened. Any attack on religious place, religious idea is faced with combined effort in the interest of religions and all are united. For example, once an ascetic of Ramanand Sampradaya published a revised Valmiki Ramayan with his own inter-pretations. This interpretation was against the established norms about their tutiliary deity Rama. This move of Swami Bhagawadacharya offended the ascetics and they unitedly opposed it. For this they also went to the court of law and got decree in their favour. For the opposition many meetings and appeals to Sadhus were made. This way we see that the organisations are working together.

No doubt, there are personal differences between Mahanths and between general ascetics of two (2) Organisations, but such differences are not obstacles in their general unity and mutual co-operation. All the ascetics assemble at the time of Bhandaras of any organisation and their unity is also seen at the time of Guru-Parvas.

Interaction Between Mahanths

The Mahanths of different ascetics Organisations are in interaction like the two Lords, Jamindars. Being the Sarvadhikari of Mutt they are the supreme authorities in the matter or Organisations. The two Mahanths interact on equality basis. If one Mahanth is of the Guru-Gaddi the other Mahanth will pay respect by touching his feet in reverence to the Guru's place, no matter if the Mahanth of Guru's place is younger than the other. He will sit at a lower Asan. But the

Mahanth of other place who is equal in Sthans will treated as an equal and sit by the Mahanth. They interact on brotherly level. Mahanth of other Sampradaya will also get equal treatment. At the time of Bhandara the Mahanths sit in a separate Panghat as per their status. The general ascetis are given a separate Panghat at that time.

The Mahanths at present are in general devoid of Sidhi and Sadhana and indulge in unnecessary bickerings. This has dragged them into worldly differences e.g. superiority complex, and showing off by expanding much at the time of Bhandaras. Very few cases are there when Mahanths have gone to court of law for solving the internal differences of economic nature.

It has been observed that the Mahanths of different organisations at Ayodhya usually visit each other in the evening and whenever they find good time for it. This shows the co-operation among the Mahanths. They all units to face any outer attack on the matter of Sampradaya or Hinduism.

Interaction of Mahanths with Other Ascetics

The Mahanths are the supreme heads of Organisations and they enjoy favourable position for themselves. Their followers ascetics are always ready to abide by the directions of Mahanths. The Mahanth distributes various jobs to ascetics keeping in view their capabilities qualifications, experiences and devotion. In the present changed pattern of ascetic Organisations, it can be said that ascetics are like employees, who get boarding and food and perform the work of organisation. The senior ascetic member enjoys superior position. In Rmanujee Mutts it has been observed that only Dwijas are taken into ascetic fold. But, among the reformist Ramanandis Mahanth initiates all caste people. They have abolished Gotra System and in place of Gotra, they call themselves Achyut Gotra. For caste identity, which is dying now-a-days, the two terms were used — Sutradhari, the persons from twice born caste i.e. Brahmin, Khatriya, Vaishya. Maladhari—the persons from unclean caste. Mahanths only appoints Dwijas as Pujari. Now-a-days Maladharis are also Mahanths, for example Mahanth of Rasik Niwas. The Mahanth pays respect to all the ascetics whether he is Maladhari or Sutradhari. Even a Parkhatriya is called by the Mahanth in respectable manner only. This is an unique picture of ascetics organisations at Ayodhya about the Mahanth—ascetic relations. The general ascetics hold very high respect for Mahanths of their Organisation.

Interaction of Ascetics with House-Holders

The ascetics from very from very beginning are in transition with house-holders, the Grihasthas, Having attained Sidhi through austere penance they were doing good to the greatest number of people by showing them the correct path of human life. Mention may be made of Dadhichi, who offered his bones to kill the devil for the benefit to humanity. Panini after achieving knowledge presented the first grammar, still considered as the best in the world, to the society. Sushrut, the first Surgeon of the world spent his entire life in treatment of patients. Manu is famous for his first law book Manusmrity, which is the base of present Hindu Law of Society. Ramanand, was first to initiate people of all caste, thereby launching movement against untouchability, the greatest social evil. Manu has mentioned in his law book that the ascetics should live on alms of Grihastha and preach them the right path of living. This notion opened the way for regular interaction between ascetics and Grihastha. The occasions of interactions between ascetics and Grihastha are many. People from rural and urban areas belonging to the Orthodox Hindus, approach these ascetics to be initiated by Guru. They believe that a Gurumukhi Hindu is sure to get place in Swarg after death. These disciples accept the Guruvachan as final judgement. They contact their Guru for all important decisions of their family like litigation, marriage, sickness, opening of new enterprise, purchase of land and construction of house etc.

They invite their Guru on all auspicious occasion in the family and give them highest regard. They pay reverence by sending Gurudakshina in cash or kind periodically or at the time of visit of Guru to their place. It has also been observed that those disciples having no issue donate their entire property to their Gurusthan. Almost all ascetic organisations are having temples within the premises where general public come in contact with the ascetics at the time of visit of temples. All Organisations at Ayodhya organises Katha-Pravachan, Ramlila, Ramayan Patha, Ramarcha Yajna, during festival time largely participated by pilgrims. These are the important occasions when Grihasthas come in close contact with ascetics. Many Mutts at Ayodhya provide residential facilities to the pilgrims.

The wandering ascetic reaches to a village, and he is welcomed by the villagers. The villagers show their eagerness to arrange Katha, Kirtan, Bhagwadbhajan under the leadership of these ascetics. The ascetic generally explains the concept of Pap and Punya, and also explains the ways of attaining Punya before he delivers lectures or Ramayan or other religious texts. It has been observed that these wandering ascetics motivate the public for construction of temples at their places. Thus, the ascetic becomes part and parcel of the village.

The ascetics of Ayodhya are mostly engaged in active social work. They extend their helping hands at the time of famine and flood. They have opened many Sanskrit Pathsalas, Homeopathic Charitable Dispensaries, Gosalas, Vyayamsala, Libraries, Research centres of religious texts etc. They are opening new Sacred Shrines which attract the mass, and this way the frequency of interaction enhances.

The Varna-Jati consideration has deeply rooted in Ramanujee ascetics who only initiates Dwijas in the ascetic fold. But the Ramanandies, the peculiar reformist have broken the boundaries of caste-system. They have accepted disciples from all castes and interact equally with them. The only consideration of caste is at the time of appointment of Pujari who should be a Brahmin. This is also because of belief in Samskara of a man. Samskara means the mental calibre and pious thinking of a person which he has learnt in pious environment of the family. The Naga or Atit or Vaishnava Akhara have fought war against Muslim of Amethi for protection of Hindu Shrine Hanuman Garhi and thereby defending Hindu faith. These ascetics activities of Ayodhya have left great impact on householders who believe that Vaishnava ascetics of Ayodhya are the real Vanguards of Hinduism.

9

ASCETIC ORGANISATION AND FORCES OF CHANGE

India is still regarded as the Spiritual Guru of entire world. The Ascetics of Vedic age were far superiors in attaining knowledge and thereby doing good for the human being. For them there were different codes of conduct and any failure meant great loss in their penance. First of all they had to procure complete influence on their limbs, and were required to keep themselves aloof from all types of worldly pleasure and luxuries. The ascetics engaged in Panchagni Tapasya are well known. Some of them lived only on water, other on wind, some on yellow leaves, others on grains fallen on ground after harvesting. Ascetics living on Kand-Mool, Fal-Ful were general. The main purpose of these was to attain Siddhi.

Time became the important factor in bringing changes among the ascetic pattern also. Ascetics like Vishwamitra, Vashishta, Bharadwaj, August and Janak went with their time. Sidhartha, Mahavir, who made arrangements for the spread of their religious ideals for the welfare of mankind, were the ascetics of same order. The foreign invasions created great confusions in this country and during the time of Tulsidas also, those who could not earn livelihood, become Ascetic. They were nothing to do with penance but they earn their livelihood only.

Comparing present ascetic order at Ayodhya with that

of Textual or Traditional Asceticism a marked change can be realised. With the advent of Ramanand, the first departure of asceticism for organised social reform appeared and since then Ramanandies were known as reformist Vaishnavas. They accepted people from all caste and class harnessing the rigidity of caste-system. Even Mohammadens were initiated into the field of Vaishnavaism and the credit goes to the Vaishnava ascetics of Ayodhya. Among the Mohammedans saints who accepted Vaishnavaism were:

(i) Sant Kalandar Sah: he came to Ayodhya from Bukhara in Middle East. His place is still at Janki Ghat.
(ii) Saint Ibrahim Sah: Son of King of Arab, came to Ayodhya. His place is at Argara, Swargdwar.
(iii) Saint Khajuhi Peer etc.

This marked the change from traditional Brahminic orthodoxy to liberal attitude. For the first time to protect religion from outside invasions the Vaishnava-Chhatuh-Sampradayas were organised into one Militant group by Swami Balnandjee in the year 1720 A.D. This was called Akhara, the details are given in Chapter-VI, of this book. The organisation of peace was completely changed when it prepared for war. The pattern formed at that time is still continuing even though the old functions have completely ceased. The study of the ascetic organisations at Ayodhya shows that almost all organisations have simplified the traditional rigidity of taxually prescribed norms to perform religious rituals. Ramanujee Vaishnavas are still maintaining the same but the Ramanandies organisations have made it easy for everybody. That is why the influx of people in Ramanand Sampradaya has strengthened the ascetic organisations. In lieu of personal Sadhana and Siddhi the Vaishnava ascetics have preferred social service. Their main aim is to propagate the essence of religion to the mass. Unlike the Shaiva Sanyasis, Vaishnavas have strengthened the Grihastha system in India. The study of Mutts shows the positive response of ascetic organisations to social change. These Ramanandi Ascetic Organisations have actively participated in National Freedom Movement. Baba Ram Charan Das and Banda Vairagi, who were hanged by British Empire for organising movement against British is well known. Sultanpur Gazatteer p. 26 has given good description about the movement led by Baba Ram Charan Das at Faizabad. Baba Girivar Das, participated actively in Freedom movement and also participated in Annual Conference of All India Congress, 1922 A.D. with many of his colleagues. Brahmachari Basudevacharya of Smarak Sadan has received freedom fighters' certificates. After Independence the Vaishnava ascetics of Ayodhya also involved themselves into politics as they believe that politics without religion is life-less. Everybody knows that there are Political Organisations of ascetics known as Bharat Sadhu Samaj and Ram Rajya Parishad, which are run by these ascetics who are politically very conscious. In general election the members of Parishad were also elected by the people in good number of Rajasthan State Assembly. At Ayodhya also the ascetics take active part and are the supporters of Jana Sangh Party now Bhartiya Janata Party. They also take part in Satyagrah, Dharana and demonstration for Go-Raksha. They have joined hands with Gohatya Andolan, Akhil Bharatiya Virakta Mahamandal which was established in the year 1945 by Swami Basudevacharya is working uniquely to develop understanding between the two sects, Shaiva and Vaishnava. They are also publishing a Weekly news Virakta since 1947. Mahanth Sri Raghubir Prasadacharya, Paramhansa Ramchandra Das, Ram Surat Saran Das were also elected as Municipal Board members of Faizabad. This leads us to conclude that even at present these ascetics aim at the national development and contribute to the same in their own way. The ascetics on present day are also involved in economic pursuits. Daan is considered as the main Dharma in Kaliyug. Therefore, the ascetics and their organisations are getting Daan from the rich people of Society and this way they have accumulated wealth in the organisations which at times becomes the subject of litigations (Case Study No. I., 3). It has also come into notice during the field investigations that the general ascetics had opened their bank accounts like Rs. 5,00,000/- and Rs. 60,000/- (Rupees Five Lakhs and Rupees Sixty thousand) respectively. Most of the Organisations are having land under cultivation at various places. The wandering ascetics are also collecting money during their visits to places and are keeping account in banks. When the amount reaches Rs. 15,000/- to Rs. 20,000/- they purchase a piece of land for making their Mutts. Approximately 2,000/- (Two thousand) ascetics at Ayodhya are having their accounts in banks and post offices, varying from Rs. 1,000/- (Rupees one thousand) to Rs. 15,000/- (Rupees fifteen thousand) and above., In many cases the ascetics are having more than one accounts and that too in the name of their Chelas. The hereditory convention also proved harmful for the ascetic Organisations. The disciple of a particular Mahanth get Gaddi together with all assets by virtue of his being a disciple, even if, he is not at all fit for the same. Many organisations at Ayodhya have been fund having contacts with their old family members and yet giving Mahanthi to their relatives. With this also entered the different types of evils of the present age. The Mahantha has his Gaddi, the Gaddi has its own property and a number of disciples. He gets free service and offerings. He has nothing to bother about and under these circumstances, he gradually enters into luxuries and become a bad name for the word ascetic. The general flow from poverty striken people also has brought worst changes. Frustrated people become Sadhus as reflected from their life histories. These people have only changed their names but not the old habits of taking intoxicants and non-vegetarian dishes. The history of Akhara establishment shows that in Medieval period there was a group rivalry between Shaivas and Vaishnavas. But now this rivalry has totally vanished though on occasions the healthy competition is still there. This competition between different Mutts, between different Sampradayas has also been seen at the time of Kumbh where each ascetic organisation tries to attract the people in its personal interest. The Ramanandies who were previously organising themselves under Jagadguru Ramanujacharya have now-a-days separated themselves and have selected one Jagadguru Ramchandracharya as discussed in the previous pages. A very new trend has emerged and that is the Shaivas, Vaishnavas and others speaking from a common platform for development of Hinduism.

The Akharas, which are based on military pattern are also suffering from evil practices like indulgence in criminal cases, theft cases, litigations etc. (See case studies No. 4, 5, 6). The physically strong Vairagies are now indulged in capturing land of others, fight among themselves for Pujarpana of temple (case-study No. 1). Some of them have been found indulged in evil deeds, disputing a question about celebrate. The foreign spies, working in disguise of an ascetic, the criminals, adopted ascetic rules, in order to conceal themselves, the smugglers, thieves, dacoits, the blind female followers corrupting the Mahantha have presented a dark picture of ascetic before society. These types of people are doing all evil deeds. In this connection, the following points are to be considered:

(i) If any Mahanth vacates his Gaddi, it must be verified, whether the successor is qualified for the same and also the management of property is done well.

(ii) Undue entrance of persons in asceticism should be strictly prohibited in the interest of the ascetic organisation.

(iii) There must be a demarcation between the ascetics interested in Sadhana and such who have taken the shape of ascetics only for getting food and cloths.

(iv) It is also a matter of disgrace that Vairagies are indulged in criminal activities, luxuries, accumulation of wealth, intoxicant and women and other un-natural habits. This must be rectified.

(v) It has been noticed that Mahanths and other ascetics are also attending canteens, chewing pan, wearing fashionable clothings, visit films (only in the night shows). These non-Samskritic habits should be avoided.

(vi) The Organisation, where Mahanth and ascetics are indulged in agricultural activities their Mahanth works like landlord and the general ascetic as manual labourers. This is a bad picture of the Organisation and it needs rectification.

All the changes noted among the present day ascetics at Ayodhya in general gives an idea that the degenerative change is marked as it is deviation from the textual prescribed form.

Conclusion

On a journey from India of the past to the present India, a conscious traveller finds himself in different diversities and at least for a moment begins to think over whether the change is for betterment? India, no doubt, has centuries back well established its position in the world due to its plain living, his thinking, lofty ideals, and miraculous achievements of ascetics.

The ascetics of India in general, and Ayodhya in particular, contributed much to the Indian (Hindu) civilisation, and for them penance was very important. The ascetics of present century maintained the old tradition, Sri Yugalanya Sharanjee of Lakshman Kila had attained such lofty position by observing penance, that even the British Empire was moved by his achievements, and offered *Mubarak Kila* now Lakshman Kila as a token of reverence. Swami Vaishnava Dasjee of Chhoti Chhawani was also the ascetic with highest Siddhi. These example show that the ascetics of Ayodhya were interested in finding the truth.

It is well-known that the contribution of ascetics to Indian civilisation is praise-worthy. The Vaishnava ascetics of Ayodhya having a good number of disciples are engaged in practising the way of life directed by the ascetics. As such the ascetics, the Mahanths of ascetic Organisations, have contributed and still contributing to maintain socio-religious-life of the general mass.

Like the ascetics of other religious places, ascetics of Ayodhya are also working as Religious Specialists as they engage themselves in performing religious rites, functions, worshipping idols of Rama with his associates reciting Rama-Nama, organising and taking part in Rama-Kathas, Pravachan, Ramarcha and other religious activities. They also attract many other people and impell them to perform several religious functions. They occasionally go with their disciples and devotees to places where such functions are being organised in which the people of locality take part. They, themselves, or through their assistants, also see that the religious performances are organised in different villages and towns from time to time. In this way these ascetics, the religious specialists, keep the religious aspects of Indian civilisation alive in social pattern. Not only this, they also take keen interest in convincing non-believing persons regarding the importance of the Hindu civilisation and India's socio-religious culture.

The ascetics are also the protectors of Dharma. It is the unique phenomenon of Vaishnava asceticism that they have organised themselves into a millitant group i.e. Akhara to fight from the external invasions on Hinduism. The very peculiar feature at Ayodhya is that the religious centres i.e. Mutta and temples are being maintained by these ascetics only. They not only preserve the religious centres, but also make all efforts to develop them. They contribute to maintain the traditional religion by describing ancient glories of the places and persons.

The ascetics do much in the field of imparting knowledge to the mass by Cultivating the Excellance of religion. They organise religious discussions and discourses in the remote villages and in this way acquaint the mass of Little Tradition with the text of Great Tradition. Being influenced by these ascetics many people of little-traditions join the fold of ascetics and in this way tradition of asceticism is continued. The Gurū-Shishya—Parampara i.e. the initiation of novites into Vaishnava asceticism moves from Guru to Shishya and contributes in expansion of Indian civilisation. The transcedental knowledge, in this way is passed from one to another. This way the continuity is being maintained. The Mahanths and ascetics are preservers of religious centres. The most peculiar feature of Ayodhya is the Mut-Temple-Continuam. All the Vaishnava Mutta cannot be imagined separately without a temple. The idea behind is that the ascetics residing in the Mutta maintain and worship Lord Rama either as Das or a Antarang-Sakhi. In both types of worship the presence of a deity at the place of worship is a must. At Ayodhya a temple without an ascetic or a Mutta without a temple cannot be imagined. An analytical study of the ascetics at Ayodhya in previous Chapters shows that:

(a) The ascetic themselves aimed at the realisation of the truth by controlling themselves both physically and mentally. They practised severe penance gradually increasing its type and degree and thereby getting full control over their senses.

(b) The achievements, on the one hand, blessed them with high powers, while on the other hand, their devotees were benefited by their penance.

(c) They realised the truth and obtained various types of knowledge through which Indian learning became extra-ordinary. Foreigners deeply interested are also accepting the fold of asceticism.

It is an establish fact that the ancient ascetics were the national ideals and their organisations played an important role in shaping the Indian Society. The ascetic organisations at Ayodhya also attract thousands of persons from different parts of the globs who are very much influenced by the ascetics' life and most of whom rigidly or liberally follow the path of life as desired and directed by the ascetic Guru. After Buddhism and Jainism, it is the Vaishnavas who still maintain the principle of Ahimsa and their followers are still strict vegetarians. In the modern time, it is the Vaishnava ascetics who have contributed much in Harnessing the Caste Prejudices by accepting the Shishya from all castes in asceticism. The ascetics belonging to untouchable castes are also getting the same status like Dwijas. The persons belonging to different language groups, diversified mode of living have been taken into the fold of Vaishnava asceticism specially in Ramanand Sampradaya. The question of untouchability, the problem of forward and backward, the distinction of rich and poor, the discrimination of learned and illiterate and all other such dismantling elements have been kept aside by these ascetics of Ayodhya and thus giving treat assistance in Social Integration. The narrowness of Provincialism and Regionalism have been discredited by these ascetics. The ascetics are also preaching the essence of Hinduism and imparting knowledge of religion all over the country and abroad. This way they are the living ideals for Popularising and Universalising the religious Hindu texts.

No doubt, the present day changes and the impact of Modernisation have also entered in this sphere. The growth of population, development of townships, heavy inflow of foreigners, poverty, development of townships, heavy inflow of foreigners, poverty accumulation of wealth in ascetic organisations and blind female followers have also proved harmful to the modern day ascetics. There are the criminals, thieves, beggars and frustrated unemployed people who have joined the ascetic Organisations to hide their crime and to get food and shelters. They are misguiding the mass and different types of evils also are given support by them. Their numbers are increasing day-by-day in the ascetic organisations, and has brought the prestige of ascetics under question. On the basis of these changes in the asceticism and ascetic organisation it can be said that the general trend of inclination towards pleasure and luxury, power and properties, involvement in dirty politics, have influenced the ascetic organisations at Ayodhya also. Many Mahanth Gaddies are holding cultivational lands and are working as land-lords and the ascetics under them are being exploited by indulging in manual work. The general deterioration overpowered the ascetic organisations of the day. If these changes in ascetic organisations are not checked, the future of ascetic organisations will be in question.

In spite of the changes ascetic organisations of Ayodhya are contributing much in social-and spiritual development. They bring different castes, class, creed etc. on a common platform and on this way they are working as important uniting force.

The ascetics are maintaining a distinct style of life and represent Transcedental Cultural Tradition and transmit the elements of Great Tradition to Little one. Many Organisations are also engaged in social work. Deep learning of traditional worship in the field of Indian culture and asceticism are being maintained and they are also evaluating the modern outlook thus, keeping remarkable balance between the old and new.

To conclude, it should be emphasised on the basis of the present study made at Ayodhya that the ascetics and their Organisations are still the vanguard of Indian Civilisation. They are doing good to the greatest number and in this way helping a healthy social growth. It can also be added that if the ascetics and ascetic organisations at present work in a traditional manner, they can be saved from external evil entries and they will surely provide a relief to the ailing humanity.

BIBLIOGRAPHY

Bagchi, K., 1974: *Sacred Performance at Ayodhya*, Master's thesis (unpublished) Ranchi University.

Bhandarker, R.G., 1913: *Vaishnavaism, Shaivism and Minor Religious System*, Straussberg.

Bhandarker, D.R., 1940: *Some Aspects of Ancient Indian Culture*, University of Madras.

Bose, N.K., 1958: *The Geographical Background of Indian Culture: The Cultural Heritage of India* (Vol. I), R.K. Mission Institute, Calcutta.

Brahmchari, B., 1965: *Chhoti Chhawani Ka Samshipta Itihas*, Bhagwadacharya Smarak Sadan, Ayodhya.

Chanda, R.P., 1920: *Archaeological and Vaishnava Tradition, Memoirs of Archaeological Survey of India*, No. V.

Crook, V., 1909: *Vaishnavism, Encyclopaedia of Religion and Ethics*, Vol. 2, p. 87 (Ed.) James Hastings, T and T Clark, Edinburg.

Geden, A.S., 1909: *Symbolism, Encyclopaedia of Religion and Ethics*, Vol. 2, p. 141 (Ed.) James Hastings T and T Clark, Edinburg.

Ghurye, G.S., 1953: *Indian Sadhus*, Popular Book Depot, Bombay.

Gonda, J., 1969: *Aspects of Early Vaishnavism*, Motilal Banarasidas, Varanasi.

Grierson, G.A., 1909: Prapati Marg: Bhakti Marg; *Encyclopaedia of Religion and Ethics*, Vol. 2, p. 151 and 539 (ed.) James Hastings, T and T Clark, Edinburg.

Hall, T.C., 1909: *Asceticism*, E.R.E., Vol. 22, pp. 87 (Ed) James Hastings T. & T. Clark, Edinburg.

Hazra, R.C., 1940: *Studies in Puranic Records on Hindu Rites* and Customs, University of Dacca (Bulletins No. XX).

Hopkins, E.W., 1895: *The Religions of India*, Boston.

Jaiswal, S., 1967: *The Origin and Development of Vaishnavism*, Munshiram Manoharlal, Delhi.

Kane, P.V., 1930: History of Dharmasastra (Vol. I), Bhandarkar Oriental Research Institute, Poona.

Karmarker, A.P., 1949: Religions *and Philosophy of the Veda and Upanishada*, Harward Oriental Series (Vol. 31).

Lala, Sitaram, 1952: *History of Ayodhya*, Prayag Hindustani Academy, Uttar Pradesh.

Law, B.C., 1954: *Indological Studies*, Part III, G.J.R.I. Allahabad.

Macdonnel, A.A., 1897: *Vedic Mythology*, Straussburg.

Marriot, M., 1961: *Changing Channels of Cultural Transmission in Indian Civilisation*, Aspects of Religion in India Society, Kedarnath Ramnath, Merut.

Oman, J.C., 1905: *The Mystics, Ascetics and Saints of India*, T. Fisher Union, London.

Radhakrishnan, S. 1970: Eastern Religion and Western Thought.

Redfield, R. and Millton Singer, 1956: *Cultural Roles of Cities*, Man in India, Calcutta.

Saraswati, B.N., 1973: *Kashi - Myth and Reality of A Classical Cultural Traditions*, I.I.A.S., Simla.

———1970: *Contribution to Understanding Indian Civilisation*, Karnataka University, Dharwar.

Seal, Brijendra, 1913: *Comparative Studies in Vaishnavism and Christianity*.

Sharma, H.D., 1941: Amarkosh (Namlingamisasan of Amar) with the Commentary of Bhatta Kaira Swamin (Ed.) Poona.

Sharma, V.P., 1974: *Vaishnava Ascetics of Ayodhya*, Master's

Thesis (unpublished), Ranchi University.

Sharma, V.P., 1987: *Urdhwapundra: Study in Symbolic Anthropology,* The Eastern Anthropologist, Vol. 40, No. 2, Lucknow.

Sharma, D.S., 1961: *Hinduism Through the Ages,* Bhartiyavidya Bhavan, Bombay.

Sinha, S.C. and B.N. Saraswati, 1978: *Ascetics of Kashi — An Anhtoropological Exploration,* N.K. Bose Memorial Foundation, Varanasi.

Srivastava, IRA 1974: *Myth and History of Ayodhya,* Master's Thesis ((unpublished) Ranchi University, Ranchi.

Tripathi, R.R., 1970: *Sri Hanuman Garhi Ka Itihas,* R.L. Gupta Book Sellers, Ayodhya.

Tripathi, B.D., 1978: *Sadhus of India,* Popular Prakashan, Bombay.

Upadhyaya, B. 1953: *Bahgwat Sampradaya,* Nagri Pracharini Sabha, Kashi.

Upadhyay, V.S., 1979: *Ayodhya in the Realm of Extra-Human A Preliminary Study of its Sacred Aspects,* R.J.R.V. (Vol. XIV), Ranchi.

Vidyarthi, L.P., 1961: *Sacred Complex of Hindu Gaya,* Asia Publishing House, Bombay.

Vidyarthi, L.P., *et. al.* 1978: *Sacred Complex of Kashi,* Concept Publication, New Delhi.

Williams, M., 1883: *Religious Thoughts and Life in India (Part-I),* London.

Wilson, H.H. 1961: Vishnu Puran (Translation and Edition), Calcutta, 1st ed. 1864-70, London.

GLOSSARY

Ashrama	:	Four (4) Stages of life according to Hindu texts, hermitage.
Awatara	:	Incarnation.
Akashvriti	:	Income from uncertain resources.
Amania	:	To clean or to cut food materials.
Akhara	:	Assembly of ascetics.
Adhela	:	A coin of British India.
Ashan	:	Individual.
Achara	:	Code of conduct.
Arati	:	Act of waving light before an image.
Acharya	:	Spiritual guide of teacher.
Brahma	:	God of Creation.
Brahmacharya	:	Celibary, one of the Four (4) stages of a man's life as texts says.
Bhog	:	Offer to God.
Bhed-Bhav	:	Differences.
Bhikshu	:	Followers of Buddha.
Bhandara	:	Community feast given by ascetics.
Bhakti	:	Devotion to God.
Bhakt	:	Devotee.
Charhawa	:	Offerings.
Chandala	:	An outcaste.
Ghhawani	:	Camp.
Dwija	:	Twice-born (Brahmin, Khatriya and

		Vaishya).
Dhup	:	Incense.
Dixha	:	Initiation.
Deep	:	Lamp.
Dana	:	Gift.
Dand-Kasrat	:	Physical exercise.
Digamber	:	A class of ascetic.
Das	:	Servant.
Dhuni	:	The continuous bonfire.
Daxhina	:	A gift to Brahmin or ascetic for his religious service.
Darshan	:	Devine visitation.
Fal-Ful	:	Fruit and flower.
Gaddi	:	Seat, office of the Chief ascetic.
Gober	:	Cow-dung.
Garhi	:	Fortess.
Guru	:	Teacher, spiritual.
Ghee	:	Clarified butter.
Ghat	:	Steps provided for bathing on the bank of river.
Homa Hawan	:	A form of Vedic worship, offering oblations to Gods by throwing Ghee, Shesamam, barley into a consecreted fire.
Hathyoga	:	A kind of Yoga practice.
Homa-Kund	:	Fire.
Jap	:	Worship by repeating sacred words.
Jhundi	:	A small unit of roving ascetics.
Kanphata	:	Nathpanthi ascetic.
Kotwal	:	Provost.
Kanthi	:	Necklace made up of Tulsi.

Katha-Vachak	:	One who narrates the episodes of God.
Kheer	:	Mixture of Rice, Sugar (or Jagari) Milk and many other edible things.
Kamandal	:	A water pot used by ascetics.
Madhu	:	Honey.
Mutt	:	Ascetic organisation or monastry.
Muni	:	Ascetic, one who meditates.
Mantra	:	Sacred Vedic words.
Mundit-Mastak	:	Had without hair.
Mala	:	Garland.
Mal-Mutra	:	Urine and night soil.
Mahanth	:	Chief of a hermitage.
Namaskara	:	To pay respect.
Naivedya	:	Things offered to God.
Naubata	:	Orchestra.
Parampara	:	Tradition.
Parivarajak	:	Moving ascetic.
Panghat	:	To sit in a line for meal.
Pravachan	:	Religious discourse.
Patti	:	Clan of ascetic.
Palava	:	Leaves of Mango tree.
Pradakhina	:	Circumbulance of a temple or a sacred shrine.
Panchamrit	:	A liquor with (Milk, Curd, Clarified butter, Honey and Sugar).
Panchgabya	:	A combination of Milk, Curd, Butter, and Urine and Dung of Cow.
Ramata	:	Peregrination.
Ramayani	:	One who teach Ramayan.
Ram-Dhun	:	Repetation or the name of Lord Rama.

Ramarcha	:	Special worship of Lord Rama.
Soma	:	A kind of liquor (intoxicant).
Savchadikriya	:	Nature's call.
Swadhyaya	:	Certain portion of a sacred work, reciting and repeating the Veda in a low voice.
Shishya	:	Pupil.
Samskara	:	A sacred ceremony.
Sarpanch	:	Chief of Judicial Committee of ascetics.
Sadgati	:	Happy state (after death).
Sadhana	:	Procedure that leads to spiritual attainments.
Tirath-Yatra	:	Pilgrim.
Thok	:	Family.
Tilak	:	Sect Mark on Forehead of Ascetics.
Tapasi	:	Ascetic.
Tayaga	:	Renunciation.
Utariya	:	An upper or outer garment.
Utthappan	:	Causing to rise or get up.
Urdhwa- Pundra	:	Up-right mark on forehead.
Upasana	:	Adoration on Homage.
Vairag	:	Without attachment (with world).
Vairagi	:	An anchorite of Vaishnava order.
Yati	:	Ascetic.

APPENDICES

APPENDIX - I

LIFE HISTORY - I

Present Name	:	Jagadguru Ramanujacharya Purussothamacharya
Age	:	54 years
Sampradaya	:	Sri Vaishnava (Ramanuj)
Name before initiation	:	Purussotham Dutt
Caste	:	Brahmin Gaur
Gotra	:	Bharadwaj
Name of Guru	:	Sri Seorahadaba

I was born at Nagarkot in Kangra district of Himachal Pradesh in a Brahmin family. I am second among my three brothers and one sister. I had my Primary education in a Primary school of my village. During my childhood I was living with my grand-father (Maternal) who was blind. I uses to read 'Sukh-Sagar' and 'Prem-Sagar' for him. Due to those impacts and hearing about the stories of Dhruwa, Prahlad the desire to become one like them developed in me from that time. One day a Sadhu of 16 years age came to my house. He was also a palmist, my mother was alone in the house so he got a good amount of donation. By seeing my hand he predicted that I will die within Eight days. I started weeping by knowing the fact and then I thought that without meeting with God I will die. This put me in grief. After two-three days being convinced by mother that the Sadhu was a fraud I came to normal. But this idea always pinched me upto ten years. In the eleventh year I was given Yagyopavit. From my early childhood I uses to keep my self alone thinking about Dhruwa and Prahlad. I was not good in plays. I did my Sastri education from Sanskrit Vidyalaya of my village. Then at the age of twenty-one I came to Banaras for higher studies. Here at Markandeswari Tirath I started Gayatri Anusthan for three years and then came to Vindhyachal to have Darsan of Vindyavashini Devi. There I met with a Mahatma, Sri Jaishankarjee Maharaj, expert of Tantric performances. I went with him at his place in the forest where he was popular by the name of Khamaria Baba. There, I stayed in a Kuti and I found peace in that lonely place. Some days passed in Phalahar then one devotee started donating flour of gram for my food. This continued upto seven months. Due to some health trouble I returned back to my home place. After recovery I went to Mirzapur, Uttar Pradesh. There I stayed at Chitragupta Mandir at Bariaghat. There I came across many Sanskrit scholars and remained there for a year. One day Markandey Maharaj visited my place. Second time I fell sick that too was for eight months. Shri Thakur. Singh, a Khatriya of the village took me to his house and rendered all his services in getting me cured. Then there only one Yogiraj Sri Shradanandjee arrived whose face was very similar to Sri Subbas Chandra Bose. In his company I learnt Yoga for one year. Thereafter hearing the name of Sri Deoraha Baba and came in his contact. One Brahmin family of Sri Deosharanjee Mishra gave me shelter at his house at Salempur. He was the scholar of Sanskrit Grammar. There I learnt Grammar from him and also there was one student Shri Deo Swarop Sastri who is now Head of Vedanta in Banaras Sanskrit University. He gave me good teaching on Vedanta. There I spent about one year. During this period I very often attended the teachings of Sri Deoraha Baba. Being influenced by his teachings I approached him to be initiated in Ascetic Cult. At first he refused and also tried to convince me that this is not good to be Sadhu. He also told that he does not require any service. Finally he initiated me by giving Guru Mantra at the age of 25 years. During those days there was a dense forest on the bank of Saryu river where Sri Deoraha Baba uses to reside, only seven disciples of Deoraha Baba were residing in that forest making separate kutis. I also started living there in a separate hutment.

Our training was very difficult. Sometimes Gurujee asked to keep standing in water, under chilling sun for the whole day. During winter nights he bends us to keep standing in the deep water of Saryu river. Only one corn was given to eat without salt, sweet etc. for one month. No one were allowed to talk with each other. Then during night he was giving preachings from 10 p.m. to 4 a.m. This process of Sadhana continued for two years. Afterwards by his permission came to Ayodhya and started study of Nyaya Darshan in Bal Mukund Sanskrit Pathasala. At that time I was residing in Badi Chhawani. This process continued for one and half years. Then left the study in the middle and went to Chhapra and remained there with one of my Guru Bhai. In the year 1954 at the time of Allahabad Kumbh many people were crushed and died, this gave me much trouble and I felt it deeply. Then I went to Bagara, Akhri and started residing thereby making a hut. After one year arranged for a Gayatri Mahayagya and went on roaming on the bank of Narmada river. Visited places like Bhiraghat, Maheshwar, Mandaleswar and stayed at those place for two months each. This way I spent one and half year then returned back to the service of Guru Maharaj. From there again went out to Barchi. There I put one cottage on the bank of Ramganga river. The villager of Sarder Nagar started coming to me for religious consultation. They also started offering kinds. People showed their great respect to me. There at Bareli I initiated my first disciple. One of them is still with me. There I also performed Yagyopavit of Brahmin boys. After two years stay at Bareli I went to Brindawan. There stayed with me Mahatma Pyare

Mohan Das of Chaitanya Gaudiya Sampradaya. Then after I also helped my Gurubhai Bhagwandasjee in construction of Vedanta Ashrama at Keshighat. After four years of stay at Brindawan left the place in 1962 at the time of Haridwar Kumbh and started study of Vedanta at Banaras by the order of Gurujee. Sri Neel Maghacharya was my Vedanta teacher. In this period only by the order of Sri Abhinava Ranganath Prakash Mahadeshik, The Rajguru of Mysore wanted to continue my study of Vedant till 1965 and then returned back to Banaras. Dwarikadhish temple was my place of residence. In 1968, a magazine Desik Sudha was published from Allahabad and I become the first editor of it. This continued upto 1975. In the middle, i.e. in the year 1971 established one Deoraha Baba Seva Sansthan. In the year 1973, Sri Deoraha Baba started Akhand Ram Jyoti. This Jyoti has been enflammed at sixty main places. In Prayag people honoured it much. In Kanpur, the Mayor welcomed the Jyoti. In Delhi the Mayor Kedar Nath Sahni welcomed it. One day the Joyti programme has also organised at the residence of Sri Gopal Swarup Pathak, the Vice-President of India. In Haridwar Kumbh of 1974 the Jyoti received a warm welcome and thousands of ascetics participated in Yajna. From there it came to Lucknow, then in various cities of Bihar in Patna-Manas Jyoti Mandir was established and Sri Bindeshwari Dube, the Health Minister become the Chairman of the Organisation. The Jyoti was invited in Nepal after that it came to Ayodhya in 1978 and from then it is here at Sugriv Tila and I am here with the Jyoti.

The present education system and teaching environment, the moral degradation of the people, the developing mass chaos pinches me much. I feel that for real peace of human being the moral and religious consciousness is required.

The present day developing caste and class differences and inter-group rivalry concerns me much. In the field of religions, the spreading chaos is dangerous for society. Therefore, I feel that one organisation of all Hindus of world can help us to minimise the same. This way we can collect money to help the down-trodden brother. If this section of society will remain untouched by our brotherly affection, it may grow to divide the community into pieces which will be a curse for humanity at large.

At present I am working to establish the following for betterment of society:

1. Establishment of Natural Hospital.
2. Establishment of Yoga Ashram.
3. To keep burning Akhand Ram Jyoti and I am also writing a book - Niskantak Marg.

LIFE-HISTORY - 2

Present Name	:	Mohanth Sri Nritya Gopal Das
Age	:	41 years
Sampradaya	:	Sri Vaishnava (Ramanandi)
Name before initiation	:	Nritya Gopal
Caste	:	Brahmin Gaur
Gotra	:	Vashistha
Name of Guru	:	Sri Ram Manohar Dasjee

I was born at Karhala Mathura in Uttar Pradesh in a Brahmin family. We are two brothers. I am the youngest. The elder died at an early stage. I had my primary education at School in Kamai Village upto Vth class then upto Seventh Class in Barsane. Passed my Matriculation from the School at Koshi Kala village. At Thirteenth year I was provided with Yagyopavit. My family members were of very religious nature. Therefore, the Sadhus from different parts used to stay at my place. This type of Satsang was a common feature of my house. Having heard the stories of great Saints and almightyness of God I started thinking about the God. Moved by the preachings, the sense of Vairagya developed in me.

On 2nd October, 1953 when I came out from my house to celebrate Gandhi Jayanti I decided not to return back again. I was very much interested to see Lord Jaggannath at Jaggannath Puri. I started for there. From Kashi I came to Mathura then to Faizabad and then came to Ayodhya. Here, I first went to Rin-Mohan Ghat had my bath in Saryu then went to 'Vijay-Raghaw' the Mutt of Acharies. There I talked with Mahanth and expressed my desire to become Sadhu. They refused to accept me giving the argument that they will not accept a person with English studies. Then from there came to Mani Ram Dasjee ki Chhawani were I met with a Saint Sri Ram Bilash Dasjee and he brought me before Swami Ram Manohar Dasjee, who gave his consent and thereby I started living with him in his Garden. After 15 days Sri Maharajjee initiated me into ascetic cult. He was of the opinion that I should continue my further study but I wanted to spent time in Bhajan-Kirtan. The Bhajan-Kirtan continued upto Six months and then by the inspiration of all other ascetics I went to Balia with my Guru Bhai Sri Ram Sewak Das and there at Vidya Bhawan, Asega, I continued my study in Sanskrit for Prathama then from there went to Kashi where stayed for two months only and then returned back to Ayodhya. Here I appeared in Prathama examination from Rajkiya Vidyalaya and stood first with State Scholarship and did my Madhyama from there. The went to Kashi and took admission in Varanaseya Sanskrit Mahavidyalaya and got the degree of Shastree. There I was residing in hostel and was also getting National Scholarship. In the meantime Sri Maharaj left the world and took abode in Saket Dham. This happened in the year 1963 then I came back to Ayodhya dropping the midway journey to Nepal. I could not meet with Maharaj as I reached three days late. On 14th day, after the death of Sri Maharaj I was given Mahanthi of this Mutt by the other Mahanthas of Ayodhya, Sri Maharaj had already selected me as his Utaradhikari in the year 1960 when he felt ill. Since that very time I was working for him. Initiating the novites on his behalf. After sitting on Gaddi the first work done by me was construction of a Sant-Niwash. Then the construction expanded with Atithisala, Bhaktashala, Gosala, Ausadhalaya. In 1965 by the inspiration of Lord Hanuman I decided to have a Valmiki Ramayan Bhawan with a Library for Valmiki Research Centre. This is going on. This will help in healthy growth of Society, moral development of the people of Nation by following the character of Lord Ram. The main aim of life is to perform Sadhu-Seva Samaj-Seva and Rastra-Seva and to do good to the greatest number.

LIFE HISTORY - 3

Name before initiation	:	Lakshmi Narayan
Caste before initiation	:	Brahmin (Kanyakubj)
Gotra before initiation	:	Bharadwaj
Citizen before initiation	:	Indian
Mother tongue	:	Hindi
Place of birth	:	Itawa (Uttar Pradesh)
Guru's name	:	Shri Ram Lakhan Dasjee
Age	:	27 years

Pujari Lakshman Dasjee was interviewed by me in his Darhia temple where he was taking rest on a cot because of light fever. I requested him to let me know the circumstances on which he became Sadhu and he was kind enough to give me the following informations.

He said "I was born in a Brahmin family and I had two brothers and a sister also. I was the eldest one and my family was very respectable when I was four years old my Mundan was performed in the Devi temple of my village. In my childhood I off and on suffered from some diseases which made me unhealthy. I could recover my health only when I attained seventh year. Then I went to a local primary school and a teacher was also engaged to teach me it home. At the eleventh year I was in the Sixth Class but I could not pass the examination. The teacher's carelessness resulted in my failure as he never tought me properly at home. In my childhood I always set with my mother to take part in worships and prayer and in this way eleven years of my life passed away.

Having failed in the examination I felt guilty and wanted to leave home and go elsewhere for this I went to my Lohar friend Shankar who was then preparing himself for Kumbh Gangasagar fair. I requested him to take me together and he gave me permission to accompany him. I could not dare to tell my parents but I started with him for the Kumbh Mela. There I saw many Sadhus doing Bhajan-Kirtans on different musical instruments. It gave me much pleasure and I listened to them daily with great enthusiasm and much delight. The fair ended and I also accompanied with a party of ascetic arrived at this place where an enquiry was made about my Guruji. Although the Lohar Shanker persuaded me to return back home, but I paid no heed to him and I did not return with him. He, however, went home and I came to Ayodhya.

Getting all informations about me my Guruji wrote a letter to my parents who came here tried their best to take me back but I was so much impressed by the Sadhus that I denied to go back and expressed my keen desire to lead life of Sadhu and worship God. My family members went back but registered sixteen acres of land of my name and informed me about the same. The land is still in my name and its produce is being used in Sadhu Seva.

He then added, listen to me here I spent five years in the business of helping the Pujari in the sacred performances of the temple as desired by the Mahanthji and only thereafter Sri Ram Lakshman Dasjee was kind enough to get me initiated. Then after I was also appointed a Pujari and both of us perform the puja co-operatively. I am very happy in this life.

(For verification I also went to the Mahantajee who told me that the information given by Pujari Lakshman Das were correct. This life history suggests that the failure of life in an immature age often compels one to leave his house and if in that course he happens to mix with the Sadhu Mandali he becomes a Sadhu).

LIFE-HISTORY - 4

Name before initiation	:	Janak Dhari Ram
Caste before initiation	:	Kahar
Name after initiation	:	Janki Sharan Das
Birth Place	:	Salempur (Bihar)
Cult	:	Ramanand
Age	:	49 years

In course of field study I meet with Sri Janki Sharan Das an ascetic and enquired into his past history. After persuading him for about one and half hour, I could get some information from him.

I talked to him in Bhojpuri and perhaps due to this dialect he thought myself also a Bhojpuria and answered my questions with a feeling heart.

He said Bachawa I was born in a very poor family and my father had died three months before my birth. Unfortunately, enough my poor father met with the tragic bus accident at Arrah town resulting in his spontaneous death. There was only my Chachhi (Aunt) who looked after myself and my mother at the time of my birth. I could go to school only. After attaining sixth year of age and that is also because I got free education there. We had nothing as our cash and kind except the two working hands of my mother. After my father's death my mother anyhow managed to get a job of nurse at a village Hospital where she worked hard and tried her best to keep the child life of her only son happy. I passed the Matriculation examination in the Second Division from the Arrah High School and have the earnest desire to prosecute my further studies but the poor economic condition compelled me to move here and there in search of a service as it was not possible for my poor mother to bear more troubles. Any how, I got a government job of a peon in the Police Office on a monthly pay of Rs. 22/- (Rupees Twenty-two) only. There I felt much that even the outsiders gave orders to me to their personal works even though I was not meant for such duties.

One day, while returning home I met with a Saint in the compartment of the train in which I was travelling. Accidentally the saint also belong to the same Caste of Kahar to which I belong. I saw everyone who entered into the train compartment paid respect to the Saint by saying Dandwant Pranam baba and like-wise. Moved by that respect I also made up my mind to become a Saint like-wise. I wanted to leave my place immediately, but the idea of my old mother was the only hindrance then. As such I thought and it was not proper for me to leave my mother alone in that age.

Two years passed and my mother also left this world. Many a person persuaded me for my marriage but I refused to marry.

When asked the reason of refusing offers of marriage the Saint replied in an overwhelmed voice No Babua Hum to Khali Mai Ke Chalte Rukal Rahlin, Hamara To Sadhue Baneka Vichar Pakka Rahl. He again laid stress on the point and continued. Bachha after the death of my mother the only idea in my mind was to become a Sadhu and the sight of the Sadhu Baba of the train and the respects shown to him by the travellers was impelling me very seriously.

Next morning I reached my office and submitted my resignation and I left the office for searching a Guru. For this I visited Brindavan, Hrishikesh, Mathura and at last came to this Holy City of Ayodhya where I got my Guru Mantra from the Sit of Vedantiji. Thus I become a Vaishnava Saint of Ramanand Cult at the age of 23 years only. For six years I stayed in the Guru Mutt and by the Guru Kripa I became famous there.

At the age of 30 years I went out for pilgrimage by the order of Guruji and travelled upto Badrinath, Tirupathi, Nasik, Dwarika, Kathmandu and other places. It took four years and then I returned back to Ayodhya. Though I was born in Kahar family and my birth place was Salempur, Bihar I am very happy now as I have became Sri Janki Saran Dasjee from Janak Dhari Ram he told laughingly. He remarked in a happy mood that he was not a Bhojpuri only then but an Indian Saint with the pious desire for the welfare of the country and entire humanity.

He further added after returning from Tirthastan I am living at Ayodhya and passing my time in worshipping God and doing religious activities. He said, "I rise early in the morning and sleep never before 11 p.m. I keep myself always either in Dhyan Puja Path, Katha Kirtan or in the works of the Mutt." He further said "This much is enough for your information Babua because we are after all Sadhus and are not interested in the detailed life history like those who are in Grihasthi.

[This life history throws light on the fact that one born in the weaker or backward class of the society in which respectful position is difficult to be attained accepts the path of Sadhu to achieve respects from the general Hindus].

LIFE HISTORY-5

Present Name	:	Baldeo Dasjee
Name before initiation	:	Baldeo Singh
Place of birth	:	Ujjain
Caste before initiation	:	Rajput

Gotra	:	Makhpavan
Age	:	38 years

Sri Baldeo Dasjee appear very clam and sweet in disposition and acted in a very noble manner in informing me about his life history.

He started speaking in this way.

I was born in a Rajput family of Ujjain and my father was a famous wrestler. My father, from my very childhood used to teach me the art of Daou-Pench and never result me to any school. His motto was Khao Pio Mast Raho and he always expressed his ideas before his friends that in the field of wrestling he would be succeeded by his son Baldeo. He further added, Babuji (my father) used to bring me in Akhara regularly on his shoulder. I lost my mother at the age of 10 years but as I was not much linked with my mother it did not give me much pain. I always received respects from the other wrestlers of the Akhara. Gradually I became a famous wrestler and became victorious in many competitions of Ujjain's Akhara.

Unfortunately I lost my father when I was 20 years old. He died in a clash with his Gotia. At that time I was out of station but when I returned back I came to know that Rajdeo Singh was the cause of my father's death. Then and there I made up my mind to kill Rajdeo and at night I went to his place with the revolver of my father inside the pocket. I entered there through the back door and saw that Rajdeo was sleeping. I gave him a foot blow on his head he awake and tried to show sympathies but I ignored all his actings and fired the bullet shot on his head. Next day I surrendered myself before the Police Officer and a case was filed against me. The case was tried in the Sessions Court but by dint of hard labour of my advocate I received a simple imprisonment of two years. I was released after two years and then I came to Ayodhya as I had lost all my attraction at my village home. Here, I spent eight (8) years at Chhatti Chhan who afterwords kind enough to initiate me. He went on saying in this way Mahajanji I became a saint and one day Mahanth Ram Khelavan Dasjee of Hanuman Garhi suggested me to join his party since then I am here. After completion of my Chela period I became a Hurdanga here my daily routine is to look after the cows of the Garhi and am fully happy here as I get my necessities of life and pass my time in the Goseva of a holy place.

(The life-history of Baldeo Singh who afterwards became Baldeo Dasjee shows how a man after committing murders and loosing all attraction of his family comes among the Sadhus and becomes a Sadhu himself).

LIFE HISTORY-6

Name before initiation	:	Yogendra Choube
Caste	:	Brahmin (Saryuparin)
Gotra	:	Kashyap
Birth Place	:	Mahai (Bihar)
Age	:	42 years.

I was born in the joint family of my grand-father. My grand-father had five brothers. They were the Jamindars of that place. The family was well to do. My mother had special care on me and there was a maid-servant to look after me.

I have been taught by my father since age of five. He had a great desire to get me educated. A teacher of middle school was appointed to teach me with other children of the family. I was not interested in studies at that time. But I used to complete mv every task, the teacher was satisfied with me.

At the age of 8 my Sacred Thread Ceremony completed. I was not interested in religious work. To see wrestling in Akhara was my interest. One day a wrestler enquired about my interest in wrestling and assured me that he will train me for wrestling when I will cross the age of 12 years. I became very happy and I could not remember how these four years passed. Now I was studied of Class-VIII. I was called by that Guru for wrestling training. At the age of 15 (fifteen) I was well trained in wrestling. At that my look was like a youngman of 25 (twenty-five) years. I had proud of it. There was none in the school who could dare to talk with me. One day a friend of mine was beaten very badly by me. But it was my fault and I realised it. I became restless at that night due to my fault. At the next morning I left my house and came to Ayodhya. I requested the Mahanths of Barantla Patti to make me disciple. He became pleased with my health. I became Chela. My duty was to wash and clean the utensils of the temple and to attend Akhara. After three years of service I entered in the second stage i.e. Hardanga. At this stage I was appointed to bring wood to be used in cooking. I became Naga after two and a half years of this service. Before this I showed my all property even my dress to the Sarpanch as it was the rule.

As the Naga, only duty was to look after Kothor and help Kothari in their works.

In the time between Chela to Naga I took part in many wrestlings at Ayodhya, Lucknow and Allahabad. I was always the winner.

So that is all about my life uptil now.

LIFE HISTORY-7

Present Name	:	Bhagwat Das
Name before initiation	:	Bhawani
Caste before initiation	:	Brahmin Kanyakubja
Gotra before initiation	:	Bharadwaj
Age	:	73 years

Guru's name : Swami Ram Ballabha Sharajee
Cult : Ramanand

I was born in a Brahmin family. I have five brothers and one sister. I was the third issue of my father. When I reached to the age of Five years, my father uses to take work from me in connection with the Gosala. He forbided me to go to School. It was my great desire that I should get educated. I started attending school. Somehow I reached the Fourth class. I appeared in the annual examination and I was unable to pass the examination. When I came to my house I was beaten badly by my father. Upto this age I was not interested to incline towards worship.

At the age of Ten years a very unfortunate event took place. It was the death of my mother. She loved me much. After this event one night I left my house and went to Nainital. There I stayed upto six months but unable to get accommodation for my study. Then I went to Banabareli within one month I left also for Ayodhya. At that time I was about eleven years old. I joined the Mutt of Swami Ram Ballabhasharanjee of Jankighat. He pleased with my work and gave me Guru Mantra. I also continued to go to the Pathshala to study Sanskrit. But it was not effective then I developed interest in music and began to play Harmonium, Tabala and Violine from different persons.

I spent about thirty years in that very Mutt. My daily routine at that time is to play Harmonium with Ramayani. At the age of forty-one years I started Tirthatan and visited so many religious places like Kashi, Badrinath, Rameshwaram, Haridwar, Hrishikesh, Kathmandu etc. I spent my twenty-two years in all those work. Then I returned to Ayodhya at the age of sixty-three years. From that time I am here. In the year 1969 by the order of the Mahanth of Janki Ghat I took the charge of this temple (Halwai temple) as Pujari. Nowadays I am spending my time in Pujan-Bhavan of the almighty. I think that this Sadhu life is the best where we worship the

God and Goddesses. Now-a-days many anti-social elements took Gurumantra and they are doing all illegal works. It is very shocking for me that the new generation like you do not use Chandan on your foreheads and not afraid of God. "Would you like to give any suggestion to new generation?" I asked "I would like to say this. New generation must attend the daily prayer, they must believe in God, they must worship God. It will give them mental strength."

APPENDIX - II

COURT CASE STUDY NO.1

Court Cases

For the Right of Pujarpana in Hanuman Garhi

Siyaram Das *Vs.* Mahant Ram Sevak Das etc.

(appellant) (Respondent)

In the Court of Additional Munsif No. 6 Faizabad

Registration No. 79/1977

The present Pujari of Haridwari Patti, Ramshanker Das is not entitled for entry in Hanuman Garhi as he is neither the Chela of Hanuman Garhi nor a Virakt Vaishnava. He is a married person and with the help of some mischievous act he entered into the temple for Pujarpana which is against the principle of Hanuman Garhi. The other Sadhus wants to kick him out form the temple and its Pujarpana so they have filed a case in the Court of above Munsif of Faizabad which is continuing since 1977. The Case is still in the court and Judgement awaited. But the claim of the Pujari is that he is a Sadik Chela of Baba Ramdas and has left his house seven years back and he is a Virakt Sadhu in the Thok of Jamuna Das that's why he has all right to enter into the temple.

COURT CASE STUDY NO. 2

Theft Case

In the Court of Special Judicial Magistrate No. 1 Faizabad

Chaturbhuj Das Vs. Mahanth Kaushal Kishore Das Baddichhawani, Ayodhya

Section - 380 IPC

Sri Chaturbhuj Das, Chela of Mahanth Kaushal Kishore Dasjee lodged a complaint against his Guru that he has stolen his materials and kept in his possession.

Case was decided in favour of Mahanth Kaushal Kishore Dasjee.

COURT CASE STUDY NO. 3

For succession — Application under Section 383 of Indian Succession Act.

In the Court of the Civil Judge, Faizabad.
Sri Raja Raghuvanswani Singh of Amanwa (applicant)
Sri Harnam Das Vedanti and others (Opponent)

Misc. Case No. 55/1975

Trustee Number - 3 Raja Raghuvana Mani Prasad Singh, 57 years, Adyakachaha Trustee Sri Janki Jeevan Trust filed a suit against the present Mahanth Harnamdas Vedanti claiming that present Mahanth has no right to change the bank transaction on his name. Because he is not trustee like previous Mahanth Sri Ram Padarath Dasjee Vedanti.

The case is in the Court since 1975 and still continuing.

COURT CASE STUDY NO. 4

Criminal Case

In the Court of Special Judge No. 1 Faizabad 77-78

On 15.7.78

Sant Ram Sharan Vs. Baba Sarju Das

Sections

323 — Quarrel
506 — Abusing
306 Attempt to murder

The case is still pending.

COURT CASE NO. 5

For Quarrel

In the Court of 1st Special Judicial Magistrate Faizabad

Chandra Prasad Singh	Vs.	Mahanth Siya Raghav Sharan Das and others

Sections

323 — Physical offence of mild nature
504 — Abusing
506 — Threatening

The case is still pending.

COURT CASE STUDY NO. 6

In the Court of First Special Judicial Magistrate Faizabad

Raghunath Das	Vs	Devi Prasad Vaidya and Six (6) others.

Ramayan Bhawan, Vibhishan Kunj

Sections

416, 417, 420, 419	Cheating and dishonesty
506	Criminal intimidation
147	Offence against public tranquility
323	Voluntarily causing hurt
467, 468	Forgery

The case is still pending.

COURT CASE STUDY NO. 7

O.S. No. 505 of 1975

For Possession — Copy of Judgement dated 22nd February 1979 passed by Sri R.C. Pandey Civil Judge Faizabad

Swami Bhagwadacharya Smarak Samiti and others (Plaintiffs)

Vs.

Akhil Bhartiya Virakta Mahamandal (Defendants)

Judgement

This is a suit of possession over Room No. 122 and House No. 3 of the map.

Order

Plaintiffs suit for possession over the Room No. 1 and Building No. 3 as shown in the map with the plaintiff is decreed defendants are allotted two months time to vacate the premises and hand over possession to plaintiffs failing which plaintiffs will have a right to get possession through court. In the circumstances of the case the plaintiffs will bear their own costs. The plaint map shall form part of decree.

Sd/- R.C. Pandey
Civil Judge
F.D. 22/2/1979

APPENDIX - III

List of Ascetic Organisations (Muthas) at Ayodhya

Sl. No.	*Name of Ascetic Organisations*	*Muhalla/Location*
1.	Vidya Kund	Mani Pravat
2.	Sita Kund	"
3.	Pauharijee Ka Sthan	"
4.	Baddi Chhawani (Baba Raghunath Daskichham)	Raiganj
5.	Tapasijee Ki Chhawani	Ramghat
6.	Bhakt Majijee Ka Sthan	"
7.	Charusheela Bag	Jankighat
8.	Charu Shila Kunj (Badasthan)	"
9.	Ram Ballabha Kunj	"
10.	Chhotee Chhawani (Man Ram Dasjee Ki Chhawani)	Basudeoghat
11.	Nritya Raghava Kunj (Shrawankunj)	"
12.	Mohinijee Ka Sthan	"
13.	Khak Chauk	Nayaghat
14.	Shiya Ballabh Bhawan	"
15.	Tulsi Dasjee Ki Chhawani	"
16.	Divya Kala Kunj	"
17.	Rupkala Kunj	"
18.	Lakshman Ghat	Lakshmanghat
19.	Lakshman Kila	"
20.	Sadguru Sadan	Golaghat
21.	Jhunjhunia Babakasthan	Jhunkighat
22.	Hanumat Niwas	Swargdwar
23.	Hanumat Sadan	"
24.	Bamanjee Ka Sthan	"
25.	Iksha Bhawan	"

26.	Badhai Bhawan	Swargdwar
27.	Viyahuti Bhawan	"
28.	Rajgopal	Shringarhat
29.	Badikuttia (Pramodvan)	Pramodvan
30.	Janki Niwas	"
31.	Chhotee Kutia	"
32.	Raghunath Kunj	"
33.	Ramayanijee Ki Kutia	"
34.	Vijay Raghav Kunj (Gujrati Baba Kisthan)	Ramghat
35.	Raghavajee Ka Sthan	"
36.	Nirmohi Akhara	"
37.	Digambar Akhara	Datuan Kund
38.	Mahavirakt Sthan	"
39.	Khaki Akhara	Shringarhat
40.	Vaidyajee Kasthan	"
41.	Hanuman Garhi (Nirwani Akhara)	Ramkot
42.	Tugal Madhri Kunj	"
43.	Mattagajendra (Matgainer)	"
44.	Mangal Bhawan	"
45.	Lal Sahab Ka Darbar	"
46.	Kanak Bhawan	"
47.	Baddi Jagah (Badda Sthan)	"
48.	Ram Gulala Mutt	"
49.	Ratan Singhasan	"
50.	Rang Mahal	"
51.	Anand Bhawan	"
52.	Faqhire Ramjee Ka Sthan	"
53.	Janmasthan (Sita Rasoi)	Vashista Kund
54.	Gokul Bhawan	Katra

55.	Tapeswar Dasjee Ka Sthan	Tehri Bajar
56.	Yadav Mandir	"
57.	Nishad Mandir	"
58.	Morab Mandir	"
59.	Jalpasthan	Jalpa Nala
60.	Santoshi Akhara	Ratnakot
61.	Mai Bada	Nayaghat
62.	Ram Sakha Ki Bagia	Ramghat
63.	Bhikhan Daska Sthan	Raiganj
64.	Rasik Niwas (Siya Dulari Kunj)	Laxmanghat
65.	Ram Rati Bai Ka Sthan	Ramghat
66.	Ramaya Dasjee Ka Sthan	Jankighat
67.	Dak or Khalsasthan	Ramghat
68.	12 Bhara Badia Khalsasthan	Jankighat
69.	13 Bhai Tyagi Khalsasthan	Nayaghat
70.	Chatuh Sampradaya Kalasthan	"
71.	Mauni Baba Ka Sthan	Ramghat

Ramanuj Sampradaya

1.	Yagyavedi	Sitakund
2.	Ramanuj Kete	"
3.	Bada Khalta	Hanuman Kund
4.	Totadri Mutt	Shringarhat
5.	Vijay Raghava Mandir	"
6.	Kaushlesh Prapancharya Mutt	Vibhusthan Kund
7.	Asarfee Bhawan	Katra
8.	Kaushlesh Sadan	"
9.	Raj Sabha Sthan	Ramkot
10.	Akahanda Ram Jyoti Sthan	Sugriv Tila
11.	Divyadesh Mandir	Rin Mochan Ghat
12.	Dant Dhawan Kund	DDK.

APPENDIX - IV

1. Sri Jagadguru Ramanandacharya
   Sri Sheo Ramacharya
   Acharyapitha, Varanasi.

2. Sri Jagadguru Ramanujacharya
   Sri Purrussothamacharya
   Sugrivtila, Ayodhya.

3. Raja Jagdambika Pratap Narayan Singh,
   Maharaja of Ayodhya.

4. Dr. Ram Mohan Mishra
   Present Heir of Maharaja
   Raj Sadan, Ayodhya.

5. Baba Ram Balak Dasjee
   Gaddinashin
   Sri Panch Ramanandi Akhara
   Hanumangarhi, Ayodhya.

6. Sri Brahmacharya Basudevacharya
   Smarak Sadan, Ayodhya.

7. Sri Paramhans Ramchandra Dasjee
   Digamber Akhara, Ayodhya.

8. Mahanth Nritya Gopal Dasjee
   Chhoti Chhawani, Ayodhya.

9. Mahanth Ram Pratap Dasjee
   Chhoti Chhawani, Ayodhya.

10. Swami Ram Narayanacharya
    Kaushlesh Sadan, Ayodhya.

11. Sri Ani Mahanth Swami Ram Kelawan Dasjee
    Hanuman Garhi.

12. Sri Mahanth Harham Das Vedanti
    Vedanti Ashram.

13. Sri Janki Sharan Madhukariya
    Charu Shilakunj, Ayodhya.

14. Mahanth (Dr.) Ramjee Das
    Tulsi Manas Mandir.

15. Mahanth Madhusudanacharya
    Asarfee Bhawan.

16. Sri Sita Ram Sharanjee, Kiladhish
    Lakshman Kila.
17. Ram Surat Sharanjee
    Gola Ghat.
18. Swami Harihar Dasjee
    Janmasthan.
19. Mahanth Akhilashwar Das
    Nirmohi Akhara.
20. Pandit Ram Raksha Tripathi
    'Nirbik,' Katra.
21. Sri Prem Dasjee
    Datun Kund.
22. Dr. Madhwacharya MA, Ph.D., LLB
    Rajsabha Sihan.
23. Baba Pagal Dasjee
    Pramodvan.
24. Sri Kaushlendracharya
    Vibhishan Kund.
25. Sri Ram Sharan Dasjee
    Smarak Sadan.
26. Pandit Ayodhya Prasad
    Janmabhumi.
27. Ramayani Ram Kumar Dasjee
    Mani Parvat.
28. Sri Uday Narayan Tripathi
    Kathavachak, Kamak Bhawan.
29. Ramshanker Pagal Dasjee.
30. Pandit Hanuman Dutta Mishra
    Vidya Kund.

APPENDIX - V

Sl. No.	*Ancient Name of Places*	*Names changed by Moughal Empire*
1.	Sidhasram	Saidwada
2.	Ramkot	Begampura
3.	Vashista Kund	Kaziana
4.	Shringar Hat	Navgajee
5.	Pramodvan	Bag Hayat Bux
6.	Rasal Van	Bag Farhat Bux
7.	Meerapur	Drabibi
8.	Sapte Sagar	Hanja
9.	Champak Van	Bag Rahim Bag
10.	Tarul Van	Bag Mirzaali Bag
11.	Rajdwar	Hamamganj
12.	Pap Mochan Ghat	Gondwara-Aj-Parsa
13.	Mani Parvat	Sheesh Pagamber (Kajeepur)
14.	Yagyasthal	Hasaanukatra
15.	Guptar Ghat	Sahadat Ganj
16.	Raghubir Nagar	Raiganj
17.	Kunj Gales	Terhi Bazar
18.	Saryu Bag	Aha-Hayat Bag
19.	Nagkesar Van	Masthan Bag
20.	Swargdwar	Saidwada
21.	Tretanath	Urdu Bazar
22.	Rinmohan Ghat	Fakriabada
23.	Ayodhya Ghat	Fakrabad
24.	Tulsibadi	Khader Ganj
25.	Ramghat	Rahimabag
26.	Jankighat	Akhatar

27.	Lakshmanghat	Khwaja Hasaan Imman Kidwari
28.	Matta Gajendra	Peer Matgonr
29.	Vishakh Van	Auliabag
30.	Chakra Tirtha	Islamabad
31.	Basudeo Ghat	Angoori Bag
32.	Kaikai Ghat	Jeenat Manjeel
33.	Sumitraghat	Akhtar Manjeel
34.	Vrihaspati Kund	Bag Bijansar
35.	Vibheesan Kund	Suthatti
36.	Swarn Khan	Suleman Bag